PAYING FOR ELECTIONS

A Twentieth Century Fund Paper

PAYING FOR ELECTIONS

The Campaign Finance Thicket

BY LARRY J. SABATO

Library of Congress Cataloging-in-Publication Data
Sabato, Larry J.
  Paying for elections.

  "A Twentieth Century Fund paper."
  Includes index.
  1. Campaign funds—United States. I. Title.
JK1991.S24   1989   324.7'8'0973   89-3637
ISBN 0-87078-247-9
ISBN 0-87078-246-0 (pbk.)

Copyright © 1989 by the Twentieth Century Fund, Inc.
Manufactured in the United States of America.
Reprinted 1991

Foreword

Public distrust of and skepticism about the nation's electoral system is widespread. The increasing costs of campaign financing have suggested to many that politics is the exclusive preserve of the rich. The simultaneous rise to prominence of political action committees (PACs) seems to allow special interest groups to determine the outcome of elections. But while calls for electoral financing reform are once again being heard, there is little consensus on what reforms are practical.

Larry Sabato, professor of political science at the University of Virginia, argues that in devising reforms there is a need to distinguish between real and apparent corruption. Politics will never be as fair and evenhanded as we might like, and a failure to concentrate on those activities that seriously injure the political system can lead to even greater cynicism among the general public. Further, he argues, there are a number of problems with campaign finance—such as the relative decline of party politics and fewer truly competitive elections due in part to the enormous fundraising advantages incumbents have over little-known challengers—that must be confronted before any attempt is made to reform the current system.

The Fund has long been concerned about the problems plaguing the political process in the United States. In 1967, it sponsored the independent bipartisan Commission on Campaign Costs in the Electronic Age, which issued the report *Voters' Time*. Subsequently, in 1970, the Fund published *Electing Congress: The Financial Dilemma, Report of the Twentieth Century Fund Task Force on Financing Congressional Campaigns*. Then, in 1984, the Fund took up the issue of PACs in *What Price PACS? Report of the Twentieth Century Fund Task Force on Political Action Committees*.

Sabato takes on the issues raised in these earlier examinations—for example, in the case of PACs arguing that unworkable limitations on their campaign contributions are senseless—and goes beyond them. Animated by a concern with strengthening the political parties and restoring public confidence in the system, he makes a series of specific policy recommendations. These include the provision of free television and radio time for candidates and parties, a 50 or 100 percent tax credit for small donations to parties and candidates, and severe restrictions on honoraria and special-interest-paid travel for congressmen.

Whether or not his package is accepted in its entirety, he has paved the way for a sensible response to a seemingly intractable problem. We are grateful to him for it.

Marcia Bystryn, ACTING DIRECTOR
The Twentieth Century Fund
March 1989

Contents

Foreword by Marcia Bystryn   *v*

Introduction   1

Chapter 1: The Misplaced Obsession with PACs   9

Chapter 2: Bad Reform Ideas That Sound Good   19

Chapter 3: The Free Media Solution   25

Chapter 4: Bolstering the Political Parties   43

Chapter 5: Other Reform Ideas That Do Some Good   59

Notes   75

Index   89

Acknowledgments

The author wishes to thank Carol Kahn, Richard Sinopoli, and Beverly Goldberg of the Twentieth Century Fund, whose valued assistance and guidance made publication of this paper possible.

Introduction

Just about everyone agrees that there is a problem with the system of American campaign finance, but there is far from a consensus about what the problem actually is, much less what should be done about it. Some reformers say that the central difficulty is the growth of special interest financing of electoral campaigns, a development represented by the rapid and massive growth of political action committees (PACs) over the past two decades. They see PAC money as buying legislative favors and as a consequence propose drastic limits on PAC contributions; a few would like to ban PACs altogether.

Some observers claim that the most vital issue of campaign finance goes beyond PACs to the skyrocketing costs of modern electioneering in general, a condition that forces candidates and officeholders to spend too much time on fund-raising and deters many good people from running for public office. These reformers want to set expenditure ceilings for all candidates. Still others focus on eliminating the barely concealed aura of corruption that is prevalent in the legal practice of giving political money—from honoraria and free trips to an outlandish "golden parachute" provision that permits retiring members of Congress to take their large unspent war chests with them.

There is at least some validity to all of these concerns. The rise of special interest politics at times threatens to create a selfish, atomized society where the generalized and superior national good is subordinated to the particularized needs of narrow, greedy, but prominent and loud groups—a recipe for disaster, with the whole becoming less than the sum of the parts. And who can deny that many officeholders spend increasingly less time on the business of governing and ever more time planning and executing their next campaigns?

Yet these descriptions of the problems that exist in campaign finance yield few carefully considered prescriptions for change. For one thing, there is surprisingly little effort expended to distinguish among the three perceptions of corruption:

Perception	Description
Real Corruption	Actual, unquestionable, illegal corruption; acts that blatantly use public office to produce private gain.
Quasi Corruption	Seeming, apparent corruption; highly suspect yet legally acceptable, or not illegal, acts.
Pseudo, or False, Corruption	Acts improperly labeled as corrupt when they are not.

These distinctions matter, if only because corruption comes in many forms and disguises. The most obvious and venal is the inducement of elected officials to violate the public trust by means of bribery or other clearly unlawful means. Bribery is, of course, the act of giving anything of value in a direct attempt to influence an officeholder's decisions. This is an all too common practice in American local politics, especially in large urban areas.[1] (One estimate is that about 5 percent of the cost of construction in New York City is attributable to bribes paid to municipal officials.)[2] Where corruption exists, it is often systematic, tolerated by the community, and permitted or even encouraged by those with the authority to stop it. The line between right and wrong, legal and illegal, is usually distinct in cases of bribery, even to the offenders. These clear-cut situations present no problems to either moral philosophers or law enforcement personnel.

Other departures from political purity, however, are somewhat less well defined. The Tammany Hall machine wheelhorse, George Washington Plunkitt, once described the difference between "dishonest graft" and "honest graft."[3] The "dishonest" variety was outright bribery, blackmail, or extortion—all activities to be shunned by the discerning, respectable politician. But in Plunkitt's view, there was nothing wrong with "honest" graft, where a politician used his connections to be "cut in" on a profitable deal, even if his post was the currency used to gain a share. A legislator could do a special favor for a lobbyist, who might then be inclined to award contracts to the legislator's business or law firm. In Plunkitt's world, good deeds, returned in kind, were the essence of acceptable political and financial advancement. Today, most such insider dealings are not only against the law but deeply offensive to the citizenry.

Bribery as well as "honest" graft debase public service and severely damage the integrity of the political system. This is *real* corruption, subject to condemnation and prosecution. There are instances in the modern world of campaign finance that clearly fall into this category, such as campaign contributions made for the express purpose of buying a legislator's vote on a specific public policy issue, or corporate or union officers who coerce political donations from subordinates.

Real corruption is black-and-white, clear, and rare. Quasi corruption is grey and better represents the political world. Quasi corruption offends the sensibilities, strikes one as wrong, and seems illegal but is not. There is no better illustration of this than the perfectly legal congressional allowance for honoraria (discussed later), which permits congressmen to pocket tens of thousands of dollars handed them by special interests. Unlike campaign contributions, these gifts need not be used for a compelling public purpose, but are made solely for the private enrichment of legislators. Similarly, lavish trips given by interest groups to lawmakers and their families (a relatively new and increasingly common occurrence) are legal but nonetheless smack of corruption. And the arrangement whereby retiring congressmen can convert massive sums in their reelection war chests into private pensions is certainly quasi corruption, legal only because congressmen themselves pass the laws.

All of these instances involve substantial use of public office for private gain; fulfillment of this condition alone should be sufficient to deem an act corrupt in the broadest sense.

Some forms of "corruption" are not corruption at all, but simply some imagined impairment of integrity. It would be false to label such acts as corrupt. For instance, it is often said that the democratic process is corrupted when wealthy candidates are permitted (as they are) to spend unlimited sums from their personal fortunes to seek election to public office. Such an argument confuses corruption with unfairness. Most people would agree that free spending by the rich gives them an advantage over less well-endowed candidates, but the Supreme Court has ruled in *Buckley v. Valeo* (1976)[4] that expenditures from one's own bank account are free speech related and First Amendment protected. Some might feel this constitutionally guaranteed unfairness is regrettable, but to label it corrupt stretches the definition of corruption to unacceptable thinness. (I am not, however, contending that nothing should be done about this inequity, and I suggest in Chapter 3 a proposal for free media time that will help level the playing field without doing violence to constitutional principles.)

Another example of such pseudo, or false, corruption can be found in the controversy over political action committees. PACs are both natural and inevitable in a free, pluralist democracy. In fact, the vibrancy and health of a democracy depend in good part on the flourishing of interest groups and associations among its citizenry. This is not to defend PACs in all circumstances; indeed, on occasion they have engaged in coercion of employees and have undertaken barely concealed bribery to secure a legislator's vote. But these specific acts, and the guilty parties, not PACs themselves, ought to be castigated.

One other point needs to be made at the outset: the *appearance* of corruption can be as damaging to the political system as the reality because it may have the same tainting effect on the body politic by increasing public cynicism and alienation. President Dwight Eisenhower's belief that politicians must be "as clean as a hound's tooth" is surely necessary to retain the citizenry's trust. It is wise for elected officials to avoid circumstances that give even reasonable cause for doubt, for example, accepting money from a PAC when an important legislative vote that affects the PAC's interests is pending.

At the same time, however, there is a corresponding obligation on the part of society's watchdogs—the news media, academics, and public interest groups—to be responsible in exercising their critical oversight function. A magnificent public service that is all too rarely performed is distinguishing between real and apparent corruption for a generally inattentive citizenry that is readily inclined to believe most bad things about politicians. Conversely, it is an irresponsible use of influence to unnecessarily add to public cynicism by labeling acts corrupt when they are not. This not only injures the political system but damages the watchdogs' credibility, hampering their ability to generate reform where it is most needed. At the least, therefore, and in their own self-interest, public overseers have an obligation to refrain from using superheated rhetoric or making unsubstantiated charges.

The current system of campaign finance, then, is not without the problems of real and apparent corruption that exist within it. But the failure to distinguish between them confuses matters and makes useful reform more difficult to achieve. In addition, there are problems with campaign finance that have little or nothing at all to do with corruption—legal, practical, or tactical inadequacies that need correcting. Among these are:

- The relative decline of party politics and, in its stead, the growth of personality and interest group politics. (The consequences of this trend will be analyzed in a later section of the paper.)
- The significant drop in grass-roots, small-donor participation in financing politics and the surge in big-dollar giving by individuals and special interests.
- Soaring campaign costs that price many potential candidates out of the market, deterring qualified people from even considering running for office. For those already in an elected office, escalating costs force them to spend increasingly more time raising money and, presumably, increasingly less time governing.
- Fewer truly competitive elections, partly as a consequence of skyrocketing costs, partly as a result of the incumbents' enormous fundraising advantage over little-known challengers. The vast majority of incumbent officeholders in national and state contests are regularly reelected with ease.
- Loopholes in the disclosure requirements for political cash. Despite supposedly strong safeguards, a growing percentage of the campaign money raised and spent is not disclosed—and hidden money is dangerous money in politics. In some instan-

ces, real corruption may be obscured; in other cases, undisclosed sums may simply encourage the perception of corruption.

It becomes clear, then, that effective campaign finance reform must confront not just instances of outright corruption but also the appearance of corruption.

How should the task be approached? To start with, the complexity and flaws of the campaign system require an admission of inevitable, partial failure. "Perfect" solutions to some financial dilemmas cause worse problems in other spheres, even abrogation of precious constitutional rights, as the example of the unlimited spending of wealthy candidates suggested. (The value Americans place on individual rights is costly in other respects, too. For instance, the emphasis on the rights of the accused guarantees that some guilty people may go free. But this is considered an acceptable price for the assurance that few innocent citizens suffer false imprisonment.)

Given this dearth of ideal answers, it is especially important that there be a critical evaluation of the various means chosen to achieve desirable ends. Unfortunately, many recent proposals for reform have lacked such rigorous review; many, in fact, are a jumble of good intentions and unintended, counterproductive consequences. For instance, those who seek to limit or eliminate PACs never really explain how in a free society this can be accomplished without damage to basic liberties and the health of a vibrant democracy. Those who want to lower campaign expenditures and thus inevitably reduce the communication flow between candidates and voters fail to take into account two realities: the first is that most voters already know far too little about politics and will probably know even less with reduced campaign spending; the second is that lower levels of expenditures will further reduce the already anemic competition in most districts, thus discouraging any but very well known challengers from seeking election.

The alternatives in campaign financing are sometimes presented as an unappealing choice between leaving a deteriorating system alone and instituting bad reforms. But there is a third option—a multifaceted agenda that addresses both corruption and other problems. It attempts to accomplish these six essential objectives in campaign finance:

1. Eliminate the major elements of real and apparent corruption from the system, thus bolstering public confidence in the political process. At the same time, items of pseudo corruption should be removed from the reform agenda to clarify and fortify it.

2. Decrease campaign costs without decreasing the volume of political communications. This will lessen the pressure on public officials to raise money, permitting them more time to work on the public's business. Citizens, however, will still have ample opportunity to learn about the candidates, since information about them will continue to flow freely and relatively generously. (The free media proposal in Chapter 3 attempts to accomplish these goals.)

3. Build up the vital stabilizing institutions of American politics—political parties. Nothing in society can substitute for the good that strong parties can do, from mobilizing support for a president's program to aggregating power in a highly diverse nation. Campaign finance laws can and ought to be structured to help revivify and restore party organization.

4. Reduce the influence of special interests without infringing on basic freedoms. No matter how important or imposing, an interest group represents not the general good but the good of its members. The two are rarely the same, although most interest groups have devised elaborate rationalizations that make such claims. In the best interests of the nation as a whole, the influence of particularized interests must be reconciled with broader objectives, in ways that are consonant with free enterprise and constitutional protections.

5. Maintain and even increase the competitiveness of campaigns. The best government usually results from healthy two-party competition. Under such conditions no candidate and no party can be automatically assured of victory. This generally results in the parties offering their most capable, impressive candidates at election time, with these candidates putting forth their best efforts on the campaign trail and in office afterward.

6. Increase public participation in campaign financing by broadening the base of small contributors. When citizens of average means are encouraged to make modest donations to favored candidates and parties, there turns out to be strength in num-

bers; the avalanche of small gifts can overwhelm even an exceptionally wealthy group of PACs or individuals. The bonus for society is that citizens who contribute money to politics, however small the sum, become more involved in the system and have a greater interest in the outcome of election contests.

Chapter 1
The Misplaced Obsession with PACs

The disturbing statistics and the horror stories about political action committees seem to flow like a swollen river, week after week, year in and year out. Outrage extends across the ideological spectrum: the liberal interest group Common Cause has called the system "scandalous," while conservative former senator Barry Goldwater (R–Ariz.) has bluntly declared, "PAC money is destroying the election process. . . ."[1]

In more and more recent campaigns, political action committees have been portrayed as the central corrupting evil in American politics. In Massachusetts in 1984, for example, all the major contenders for the U.S. Senate in both parties refused to take PAC money, and one candidate even got his Democratic opponent to sign a statement pledging to resign his seat in Congress should he "ever knowingly accept and keep a campaign contribution from a political action committee."[2]

Candidates from Maine to California have scored points by forswearing the acceptance of PAC gifts earlier and more fervently than their opponents. The Democratic party included in its 1984 national platform a call for banning PAC funds from all federal elections,[3] despite its aggressiveness in attracting PAC money to itself and its candidates.

PAC-bashing is undeniably a popular campaign sport,[4] but the "big PAC attack" is an opiate that obscures the more vital concerns and problems in campaign finance. PAC excesses are merely a symptom of other serious maladies in the area of political money, but the near-obsessive focus by public interest groups and the news media on the PAC evils has diverted attention from more fundamental matters. The PAC controversy, including the charges most frequently made against them, can help explain why PACs are best described as agents of pseudo corruption.[5]

The PAC Era

While a good number of PACs of all political persuasions existed prior to the 1970s, it was during that decade of campaign reform that the modern PAC era began. Spawned by the Watergate-inspired revisions of the campaign finance laws, PACs grew in number from 113 in 1972 to 4,196 by 1988, and their contributions to congressional candidates multiplied more than fifteenfold, from $8.5 million in 1971–72 to $130.3 million in 1985–86.

The rapid rise of PACs has engendered much criticism, yet many of the charges made against political action committees are exaggerated and dubious. While the widespread use of the PAC structure is new, special interest money of all types has always found its way into politics. Before the 1970s it simply did so in less traceable and far more disturbing and unsavory ways. And while, in absolute terms, PACs contribute a massive sum to candidates, it is not clear that there is proportionately more interest-group money in the system than before. As political scientist Michael Malbin has argued, we will never know the truth because the earlier record is so incomplete.[6]

The proportion of House and Senate campaign funds provided by PACs has certainly increased since the early 1970s, but individuals, most of whom are unaffiliated with PACs, together with the political parties, still supply about three-fifths of all the money spent by or on behalf of House candidates and three-quarters of the campaign expenditures for Senate contenders. So while the importance of PAC spending has grown, PACs clearly remain secondary as a source of election funding. PACs, then, seem rather less awesome when considered within the entire spectrum of campaign finance.

Apart from the argument over the relative weight of PAC funds, PAC critics claim that political action committees are making it more expensive to run for office. There is some validity to this assertion. Money provided to one candidate funds the purchase of campaign tools that the other candidate must match in order to stay competitive.

In the aggregate, American campaign expenditures seem huge. In 1988, the total amount spent by all U.S. House of Representatives candidates taken together was about $256 million, and the campaign cost of the winning House nominee averaged over $392,000. Will Rogers's 1931 remark has never been more true: "Politics has got so expensive that it takes lots of money to even get beat with."

Yet $256 million is far less than the annual advertising budgets of many individual commercial enterprises. These days it is expensive to communicate, whether the message is political or commercial. Television time, polling costs, consultants' fees, direct-mail investment, and other standard campaign expenditures have been soaring in price, over and above inflation.[7] PACs have been fueling the use of new campaign techniques, but a reasonable case can be made that such expenses are necessary, and that more and better communication is required between candidates and an electorate that often appears woefully uninformed about politics. PACs therefore may be making a positive contribution by providing the means to increase the flow of information during elections.

PACs are also accused of being biased toward the incumbent, and except for the ideological committees, they do display a clear and overwhelming preference for those already in office. But the same bias is apparent in contributions from individuals, who ask the same reasonable, perhaps decisive, economic question: Why waste money on contenders if incumbents almost always win? On the other hand, the best challengers—those perceived as having fair-to-good chances to win—are usually generously funded by PACs. Well-targeted PAC challenger money clearly helped the GOP win a majority in the U.S. Senate in 1980, for instance, and in turn aided the Democrats in their 1986 Senate takeover.

The charge that PACs limit the number of strong challengers is true, because by giving so much money so early in the race to incumbents, they deter potential opponents from declaring their candidacies. On the other hand, the money that PACs channel to competitive challengers late in the election season may actually help increase the turnover of officeholders on election day. PAC money also tends to invigorate competitiveness in open-seat congressional races where there is no incumbent.

One line of attack on PACs that seems fairly justified is the feeling that these important components of our democratic political system are themselves undemocratic in some respects. For example, in some cases their candidate selection process completely severs the connecting link between contributor and candidate. As political scientist David Adamany has noted, this condition is most apparent in many of the politically ideological nonconnected PACs, whose lack of a parent body and whose freestyle organization make them accountable to no one and responsive mainly to their own whims.[8] Leaders of ideological PACs, however, insist that their committees are still democratic, since contributors will simply stop giving if dissatisfied with the PACs' candidate choices.

But ideological PACs raise most of their money by direct mail, which means that the average donor's only source of information about the PAC's activities is their own communication, which, not surprisingly, tends to be upbeat and selective in reporting the committee's work. Moreover, as political scientist Frank Sorauf has stressed, since direct mail can succeed with only a 2 to 5 percent response rate, and since prospecting for new donors is continuous, decisions by even a large number of givers to drop out will have little impact on PAC fundraising.[9]

Ideological PACs are not alone in following undemocratic practices. When the AFL-CIO overwhelmingly endorsed Democrat Walter Mondale for president in 1983, thereby making available to him the invaluable resources of most labor PACs, a CBS News/*New York Times* poll showed that less than a quarter of the union members interviewed had their presidential preferences solicited in any fashion.[10] If a representative sampling had taken place, the AFL-CIO might not have been so pro-Mondale, since the CBS/*Times* poll indicated that Mondale was not favored by a majority of the respondents and was in fact in a statistical dead heat with Senator John Glenn (D–Ohio) for a plurality edge.

Nor can many corporate PACs be considered showcases of democracy. In a few PACs the chief executive officers completely rule the roost, and in many the CEOs have inordinate influence on PAC decisions.

PAC Money and Congressional "Corruption"

The most serious charge leveled at PACs is that they succeed in buying the votes of legislators on issues important to their individual constituencies. It seems hardly worth arguing that many PACs are shopping for congressional votes and that PAC money buys access, or opens doors, to congressmen. But the "vote-buying" allegation is generally not supported by a careful examination of the facts.[11] PAC contributions do make a difference, at least on some occasions, in securing access and influencing the course of events, but those occasions are not nearly as frequent as anti-PAC spokesmen, even congressmen themselves, often suggest.

PACs affect legislative proceedings to a decisive degree only when certain conditions prevail. First, the less visible the issue, the more likely that PAC funds can change or influence congressional votes. A corollary is that PAC money has more effect in the early stages of the legislative process, such as agenda setting and votes in subcommittee meetings, than in later and more public floor deliberations. Press, public, and even "watchdog" groups are not nearly as attentive to initial legislative proceedings.

PAC contributions are also more likely to influence the legislature when the issue is specialized and narrow, or unopposed by other organized interests. PAC gifts are less likely to be decisive on broad national issues such as American policy in Nicaragua or the adoption of a Star Wars missile defense system. But the more technical measures seem tailor-made for the special interests. Additionally, PAC influence in Congress is greater when large PACs or groups of PACs (such as business and labor PACs) are allied. In recent years, despite their natural enmity, business and labor have lobbied together on a number of issues, including defense spending, trade policy, environmental regulation, maritime legislation, trucking legislation, and nuclear power.[12] The combination is a weighty one, checked in many instances only by a tendency for business and labor in one industry (say, the railroads) to combine and oppose their cooperating counterparts in another industry (perhaps the truckers and teamsters).

It is worth stressing, however, that most congressmen are *not* unduly influenced by PAC money on most votes. The special conditions simply do not apply to most legislative issues, and the overriding factors in determining a legislator's votes include party

affiliation, ideology, and constituents' needs and desires. Much
has been made of the passage of large tax cuts for oil and business interests in the 1981 omnibus tax package. The journalist
Elizabeth Drew said there was a "bidding war" to trade campaign
contributions for tax breaks benefiting independent oil producers.[13]
Ralph Nader's Public Citizen group charged that the $280,000 in
corporate PAC money accepted by members of the House Ways
and Means Committee helped to produce a bill that "contained
everything business ever dared to ask for, and more."[14] Yet as
Robert Samuelson has convincingly argued, the "bidding war"
between Democrats and Republicans was waged not for PAC
money but for control of a House of Representatives sharply divided
between Reaganite Republicans and liberal Democrats, with conservative "boll weevil" Democrats from the southern oil states as
the crucial swing votes.[15] The Ways and Means Committee actions
cited by Nader were also more correctly explained in partisan
terms. After all, if these special interests were so influential in
writing the 1981 omnibus tax package, how could they fail so completely to derail the much more important (and, for them, threaten-
ing) tax reform legislation of 1986?

If party loyalty can have a stronger pull than PAC contributions,
then surely the views of a congressman's constituents can also
take precedence over those of political action committees. If an
incumbent is faced with choice of either voting for a PAC-backed
bill that is very unpopular in his district or forgoing the PAC's
money, the odds are that any politician who depends on a majority of votes to remain in office is going to side with his constituency and vote against the PAC's interest. PAC gifts are merely a
means to an end: reelection. If accepting money will cause a candidate embarrassment, then even a maximum donation will likely be rejected. The flip side of this proposition makes sense as
well: if a PAC's parent organization has many members or a major
financial stake in the congressman's home district, he is much
more likely to vote the PAC's way—not so much because he receives
PAC money but because the group accounts for an important part
of his electorate. Does a U.S. senator from a dairy state vote for
dairy price supports because he received a significant percentage
of his PAC contributions from agriculture, or because the farm
population of his state is relatively large and politically active?

When congressmen vote the National Rifle Association's preferences is it because of the money the NRA's PAC distributes, or
because the NRA, unlike gun-control advocates, has repeatedly
demonstrated the ability to produce a sizable number of votes in
many legislative districts?

If PACs have appeared more influential than they actually are,
it is partly because many people believe legislators are looking
for opportunities to exclaim (as one did during the Abscam scan-
dal) "I've got larceny in my blood!" It is certainly disturbing that
the National Republican Congressional Committee believed it
necessary to warn its PAC-soliciting candidates: "Don't *ever* suggest to the PAC that it is 'buying' your vote, should you get
elected."[16] Yet knowledgeable Capitol Hill observers agree that
there are few truly corrupt congressmen. Simple correlations notwithstanding, when most legislators vote for a PAC-supported bill,
it is because of the *merits* of the case, or the entreaties of their
party leaders, peers, or constituents, and not because of PAC money.

When the PAC phenomenon is viewed in the broad perspective of
issues, party allegiance, and constituent interests, it is clear that
merit matters most in the votes most congressmen cast. It is naive
to contend that PAC money never influences decisions, but it is
unjustifiably cynical to believe that PACs always, or even usually, push the voting buttons in Congress.

PACs in Perspective

As the largely unsubstantiated "vote-buying" controversy suggests,
PACs are often misrepresented and unfairly maligned as the embodiment of corrupt special interests. Political action committees
are a contemporary manifestation of what James Madison called
"factions." In his *Federalist, No. 10,* Madison wrote that through
the flourishing of these competing interest groups, or factions,
liberty would be preserved.[17]

In any democracy, and particularly in one as pluralistic as the
United States, it is essential that groups be relatively unrestricted
in advocating their interests and positions. Not only is that the
mark of a free society, it also provides a safety valve for the competitive pressures that build on all fronts in a capitalistic democracy. And it provides another means to keep representatives
responsive to legitimate needs.

This is not to say that all groups pursue legitimate interests, or that vigorously competing interests ensure that the public good prevails. The press, the public, and valuable watchdog groups such as Common Cause must always be alert to instances in which narrow private interests prevail over the commonweal—occurrences that generally happen when no one is looking.

Besides the press and various public interest organizations, there are two major institutional checks on the potential abuses wrought by factions, associations, and now PACs. The most fundamental of these is regular free elections with general suffrage. As Tocqueville commented:

> Perhaps the most powerful of the causes which tend to mitigate the excesses of political association in the United States is Universal Suffrage. In countries in which universal suffrage exists, the majority is never doubtful, because neither party can pretend to represent that portion of the community which has not voted.
>
> The associations which are formed are aware, as well as the nation at large, that they do not represent the majority: this is, indeed, a condition inseparable from their existence; for if they did represent the prepondering power, they would change the law instead of soliciting its reform.[18]

Senator Robert Dole (R–Kan.) has said, "There aren't any poor PACs or Food Stamp PACs or Nutrition PACs or Medicare PACs,"[19] and PAC critics frequently make the point that certain segments of the electorate are underrepresented in the PAC community. Yet without much support from PACs, there are food stamps, poverty and nutrition programs, and Medicare. Why? Because the recipients of governmental assistance constitute a hefty slice of the electorate, and *votes matter more than dollars to politicians.* Furthermore, many citizens *outside* the affected groups have also made known their support of aid to the poor and elderly—making yet a stronger electoral case for these PAC-less programs.

The other major institution that checks PAC influence is the two-party system. While PACs represent particular interests, the political parties build coalitions of groups and attempt to represent a national interest. They arbitrate among competing claims, and they seek to reach a consensus on matters of overriding importance to the nation. The parties are one of the few unifying forces in an exceptionally diverse country.

If interest groups and their PACs are useful to a functioning democracy, then political parties are essential. Yet just as PACs began gathering strength in the 1970s, the parties began a steady decline in power. In the past decade the rehabilitation of the party system has begun, but there is a long way to go. A central goal of the campaign financing reform agenda should be to strengthen the political parties, and to grant them a kind of "most favored nation" preferential status in the machinery of elections and campaign finance. Reforms to bolster the parties will also serve to temper the excesses of PACs by reducing their proportional impact on the election of public officials.

However limited and checkmated by political realities PACs may be, they are still regarded by a skeptical public as thoroughly unsavory. PACs have become the embodiment of greedy special interest politics, rising campaign costs, and corruption. It does not seem to matter that most experts in the field of campaign finance take considerable exception to the prevailing characterization of political action committees. PACs have become, in the public's mind, a powerful symbol of much that is wrong with America's campaign process, and candidates for public office naturally manipulate this symbol as well as others for their own ends. It is a circumstance as old as the Republic.

PACs, however, have done little to change their image for the better. Other than the business-oriented Public Affairs Council, few groups or committees have moved to correct one-sided press coverage or educate the public on campaign financing's fundamentals. In fact, many PACs fuel the fires of discontent by refusing to defend themselves while not seeming to care about appearances. Giving to both candidates in the same race, for example—an all-too-common practice—may be justifiable in theory, but it strikes most people as unprincipled, rank influence purchasing. Even worse, perhaps, are PACs that "correct their mistakes" soon after an election by sending a donation to the winning, but not originally PAC-supported, candidate. In the seven 1986 U.S. Senate races where a Democratic challenger defeated a Republican incumbent, there were 150 instances in which a PAC gave to the GOP candidate *before* the election and to the victorious Democrat once the votes were counted.[20] These practices PACs themselves should stop. Every PAC should internally ban double giving, and there should be a moratorium on gifts to previously opposed candidates until at least the halfway point of the officeholder's term.

Whether PACs undertake some necessary rehabilitative steps or not, any fair appraisal of their role in American elections must be balanced. PACs are neither political innocents nor selfless civic boosters. But, neither are they cesspools of corruption and greed, nor modern-day versions of Tammany Hall.

PACs will never be popular with idealistic reformers because they represent the rough, cutting edge of a democracy teeming with different peoples and conflicting interests. Indeed, PACs may never be hailed even by natural allies; it was the business-oriented *Wall Street Journal*, after all, that editorially referred to Washington, D.C., as "a place where politicians, PACs, lawyers, and lobbyists for unions, business or you-name-it shake each other down full time for political money and political support."[21]

Viewed in perspective, the root of the problem in campaign finance is not PACs; it is money. Americans have an enduring mistrust of the mix of money (particularly business money) and politics, as Finley Peter Dunne's Mr. Dooley revealed:

> I niver knew a pollytician to go wrong ontil he'd been contaminated be contact with a business man. . . . It seems to me that th' only thing to do is to keep pollyticians an' business men apart. They seem to have a bad infloonce on each other. Whiniver I see an alderman an' a banker walkin' down th' street together I know th' Recordin' Angel will have to ordher another bottle iv ink.[22]

As a result of the new campaign finance rules of the 1970s, political action committees superceded the "fat cats" of old as the public focus and symbol of the role of money in politics, and PACs inherited the suspicions that go with the territory. Those suspicions are valuable because they keep the spotlight on PACs and guard against undue influence. It may be regrettable that such supervision is required, but human nature—not PACs—demands it.

Chapter 2
Bad Reform Ideas That Sound Good

Few fields have attracted as many proposals for reform as campaign finance. As disturbing as the abuses of political money have been, however, some of the proposed reforms will prove useless or, even worse, counterproductive. These siren songs of bad ideas that sound good should be identified in order to be resisted.

PAC Limits

Foremost among the currently popular proposals for campaign finance reform is limiting the amount of PAC money any member of Congress may accept. A number of legislative proposals have been made to restrict a congressional candidate's PAC total to a fixed amount ($10,000 in the case of the Obey-Railsback bill, which passed the House but not the Senate in 1979,[1] and $100,000 in the proposal by Senator David Boren (D–Okla.) that was under consideration, but not passed, in 1986).[2] Like many reforms, it has a certain superficial appeal, but the hidden costs and consequences of the proposal are enormous and destructive.

The effects of a limitation on PAC gifts make it a most undesirable innovation. First of all, limits would aid incumbents. While it is true that incumbents as a group raise far more PAC money than do challengers, in *competitive* races (where there is a good chance for the incumbent to lose) challengers sometimes match or outraise incumbents among PACs, and that money is usually much more useful to a little-known challenger than to a well-known incumbent. A cap on PAC gifts would reassure incumbents

19

that, should they find themselves in electoral difficulty, their challengers will have less chance to raise enough money to defeat them. The "PAC cap" may in reality be a "challenger cap."

Limitations on PAC gifts would also help wealthy candidates. Currently, any candidate can spend unrestricted personal funds on his own election; any reduction of an opponent's assets would thus obviously add to the power of the wealthy candidate. It is ironic, in light of the support for PAC limits by labor-oriented Democrats, that a PAC cap is likely to hurt labor and Democratic candidates more than the business interests and Republicans. (Democratic candidates depend on PAC funds more heavily than Republicans because the Democratic party cannot supply them with as much money as the financially healthy Republican party can offer its nominees.)

Some PAC-limitation proposals (such as Senator Boren's) have called for reducing the maximum gift of $5,000 per election. This is another move sure to hurt labor disproportionately, since labor PACs tend to "max out" (give the maximum allowable donation) far more frequently than corporate and trade committees. (In fact, this type of PAC limitation has already occurred as a result of inflation: the 1974 gift of $5,000 has now been reduced in value by more than half.)

The most disturbing consequence of further limits on PAC contributions would be an inevitable increase in independent expenditures, which constitute the least accountable form of political spending. In addition, these contributions are often viciously negative in tone and should hardly be encouraged by the system of campaign finance.

PACs are established organizations with the proven ability to raise money, and if their direct contributions are restricted, they will find other useful ways to spend their funds. Reformers may be able to squeeze PAC cash out of candidates' election accounts, but they will not succeed in forcing PAC money out of the political system. Other activities will simply come to the fore, such as undisclosed "soft money" gifts to parties in states without restrictions on corporate or union treasury contributions, Washington lobbying campaigns, and political education and involvement programs galore. No doubt, encouragement of large individual gifts from PAC-affiliated persons would become widespread, too.

Such donations, of course, are not as easily traceable. As the Democratic Congressional Campaign Committee's former director Martin D. Franks once speculated, "With a PAC limit, instead of getting one check from Lockheed corporation's PAC we'll get five $1,000 checks from housewives in the San Fernando Valley with no mention that their spouses are executives with Lockheed. In that sense PACs serve an efficient bookkeeping and disclosure purpose."[3] The reform advocate, Senator Boren, is himself a good case study. Boren virtuously refuses all PAC money, but a detailed *Campaign Practices Reports* investigation revealed that fully a quarter of Boren's million-dollar war chest raised in 1983 and 1984 came from executives and employees of the energy and banking industries.[4] The total was probably larger, because many contributions from "homemakers" who were difficult to identify probably were made by women related to the executive contributors.

Michael Dukakis refused all PAC money in his 1988 Democratic presidential nomination race. But the $24 million he raised by the end of the primaries came primarily from the same individuals and groups that form PACs. A *Washington Post* analysis of the Dukakis campaign's financial records showed that $3 million came from Greek-Americans; $400,000 from lawyers in Massachusetts (many of whose firms conducted business with the state as bond or corporate counsel); $98,000 from employees of Wall Street brokerage and investment firms; and similar contributions from other interested sources.[5]

If PAC money is slightly tainted, self-interested money, then why is money given individually from members of the same groups innocent? In one sense, individual gifts are actually more dangerous, because they are considerably harder for the news media to identify, aggregate, and publicize—assuming, as I do, that public exposure helps to minimize the danger of hidden influence peddling.

Finally, an overall PAC limit might increase the chances that legislative votes could be swayed by PAC gifts. If both the railroads and the trucking industry, for instance, tried to make a contribution to a congressman, but only the railroads succeeded before the incumbent's PAC limit was reached, might not the legislator be more beholden to railroad interests than to truckers as a result of this limitation? Allowing the congressman to accept donations from both the railroads and their natural competitors maintains some balance among competing interests.

One of the leading PAC critics, Representative David Obey (D–Wis.), has dismissed the argument that "limiting PACs is futile because there will always be ways to circumvent the restrictions." He said that is like saying, "Don't cure heart disease, because the guy might get cancer."[6] But considering all the problems that would be introduced by PAC limits, a better medical analogy might be: Don't use a drug with potentially lethal side effects to cure a cold.

Spending Ceilings

For many of the same reasons, the frequent call for spending ceilings in congressional races is a bad reform idea that sounds good.[7] On the surface of it, it is undeniably an attractive proposal. If we are concerned about the "obscene" levels of expenditure in House and Senate races, say the reformers, then let us set a maximum amount that can be spent.

The question is, who would determine the ceilings? The Congress, of course—a body composed of 535 incumbents who are fervently convinced of the worthiness of their own reelections. It is in their electoral interests to set the ceilings as low as possible. After all, the incumbents already have high name recognition, purchased with lavish spending during previous campaigns, and with hundreds of thousands of dollars of taxpayers' money (via congressional staffs, the frank, mobile offices, constituency services, and so forth) during their years in office.[8] The average challenger, then, begins his or her campaign perhaps millions of dollars behind the incumbent in overall real spending. Major expenditures are necessary to compensate and to compete.

The fact is, therefore, expenditure ceilings, in most circumstances, will favor incumbents and make it even more difficult for challengers to defeat entrenched legislators. While electorally threatened congressmen may disagree, the American political and governmental system is heavily weighted toward incumbents—too much so, in fact. With more than 92 percent of incumbent U.S. House members who seek another term regularly reelected (98 percent in 1986 and 1988), the last thing we ought to do is to discourage competition.

Consider also these points:

- Ceilings like PAC caps will not stop or even slow campaign expenditures; they will merely redirect the flow and channels of money. If individuals and PACs are prohibited from giving to a candidate directly (after the spending ceiling is reached), they will find ways to give indirectly. Specifically, we might again expect an increase in independent expenditures that are hard to account for and often applied in negative ways. Once more, unintended and undesirable consequences can result from well-intended campaign finance reform.

- Inevitably, ceilings will lead to creative accounting practices and other methods that will have the effect of "stretching" the limits. This has already occurred at the presidential level.[9] The effect is to undermine respect for the campaign finance system generally. Why build into the law artificial devices that almost inevitably encourage noncompliance and lead to barely legal cheating?

- Ceilings designed to reduce special interest influence on government may actually increase the power of some interests at the expense of others. Ceilings would favor the large, organized interests that are in a position to contribute early in an election cycle, before the ceiling for a given candidate is reached. Smaller groups, or those that lack capital early in the election cycle, may be forbidden from contributing directly to a candidate. Since officeholders are especially likely to give access to those who have donated money to their election campaigns, spending ceilings may also have the unintended consequence of granting more access to the "haves" and less to the "have nots."

Nonresident Contributions

A third example of a "bad idea that sounds good" comes from Philip M. Stern, founder of the "Citizens Against PACs" organization. Stern has proposed a ban on congressional campaign contributions by nonresidents of the candidate's district or state.[10] He declares his rule to be simply, "If you can't vote for a candidate, you can't give money to him/her." Bluntly put, the rule is intended to stop interest groups and individuals residing outside a congressman's bailiwick from "buying a piece" of him or her via campaign money. The arguments made earlier to rebut the notion that campaign donations buy legislative votes certainly apply here, but other objections can be made to Stern's proposition as well. First, it mistakenly assumes that all congressmen, equally elected, are in fact equal. To the contrary, the seniority system makes some congressmen far more powerful than others; committee and key subcommittee chairmen, ranking minority members, and legislative officers wield most of the authority and make most of the decisions.

Moreover, in each policy area, a handful of senior members belonging to the appropriate committee in each house of Congress call the shots on that subject, and thereby influence decisions on issues that affect *all* Americans, not just those of constituents. So how can a citizen with a vital interest in a certain policy who resides outside the districts of the relevant congressmen make an opinion heard? His or her own legislator—perhaps a less senior member assigned to other committees—can be of only marginal help, at best. Granted, nothing would stop a citizen from moving to a powerful congressman's district, or taking several months' leave to travel to the district to work for or against a senior legislator's reelection, but these are certainly not practical solutions for most people. Instead, it makes perfect sense for a citizen who is concerned about a particular policy to contribute money to incumbent congressmen or their opponents whatever their geographical locations. Liberals who back the Stern proposal would have been prohibited from contributing to anti-Vietnam War candidates throughout the nation in the 1960s and early 1970s. Conservatives who oppose abortion would be forbidden to give money to opponents of the Judiciary Committee legislators who may be blocking votes on anti-abortion bills.

Just as all legislators are not equal, congressional districts and states also lack equivalence: some are richer lodes of campaign cash than others. Incumbents just about everywhere have access to sufficient political money, but the same is not true for challengers. In impoverished inner-city districts or small, poor rural states many challengers would be starved for funds without an infusion of money from richer terrain. Stern's proposal, like the others discussed earlier, might have the effect of making some incumbents' tenures even more secure than they already are.

Chapter 3
The Free Media Solution

Campaign outlays seem staggeringly high. Indeed, the average major-party House candidate in 1986 was forced to raise nearly $3,500 a week for a full year, and the average major-party Senate candidate almost $9,500 a week for *two* full years.[1] The fundraising pressure on candidates is thus great, and increasing with each new election cycle. But, as suggested earlier, when considered in the context of consumer product advertising, political expenditures are less than overwhelming. The $451 million spent by the 1,873 candidates for House and Senate seats over two years (1985 and 1986) is well under the *annual* advertising budget of a single large corporation, Procter and Gamble.[2] Many other examples could also be cited. Surely, selecting a nation's political leadership is more important than selling toothpaste and toilet paper. A cynic could claim that the American public probably knows more about brand name household products than it does about most leading politicians or policy issues; survey after survey reveals the electorate's ignorance of the names and substance of politics.

Given the obvious need for *more* political communication and education, it hardly makes sense to spend *less* on the election process. As argued earlier, a limitation on the total amount candidates can spend would reduce competition by hurting some challengers in key marginal races where the incumbent is threatened. At the same time, society has an interest in reducing fundraising pressures on its candidates and officeholders so they can (theoretically at least) spend more time on the substance of governing and campaigning.

These seemingly contradictory goals can be reconciled and achieved. The reasonable solution is this: Instead of attempting to lower expenditures artificially, we ought to subtract from actual campaign costs. In many districts and states, costs can be slashed substantially simply by reclaiming a few advertising hours of the public's airwaves from broadcasters.

Campaign Spending on Media Time

The National Association of Broadcasters (NAB) released a study[3] in 1987 that claimed the previous year's congressional candidates had spent 24.3 percent of their total budgets on buying television and radio advertising time—nearly $100 million in all.[4] Candidates for the House of Representatives spent 15.8 percent of their war chests, while U.S. Senate contenders devoted fully 34 percent of their campaign cash to television and radio.

As enormous as this sum is, the NAB study almost certainly underestimated the total.[5] It was in the interest of broadcasters to underplay media expenditures and thus deflect some of the legislative concern and scrutiny about rising campaign costs. Ambiguous expenditures in the Federal Election Commission reports, for example, were apparently discounted by the NAB in many cases, and questionable guesswork was employed in categorizing some costs. Important expenditures directly connected to time buying (such as staff and travel costs needed to purchase airtime) were excluded. And most importantly, all House races were lumped together—unopposed, lightly opposed, moderately contested, and highly contested, and rural and urban. House races in large urban markets rarely afford much television advertising because of high costs, and uncompetitive or unopposed races require little, if any, media expenditure. So this overall averaging significantly understates media costs in many key marginal districts where competition is keen. Most experts in the field of campaign costs believe that, at a minimum, 30 to 40 percent of all campaign dollars raised are devoured by the broadcasters for airtime; in the 1986 congressional contest this amounted to between $135 million and $180 million.[6]

The estimates of media expenditures are much more precise at the presidential level due to the careful accounting and intense scrutiny that the spending of public funds entails. In general election contests for the White House, media advertising time and associated costs consume up to half or more of the entire campaign budget. In 1980 Ronald Reagan spent about half of his $29.4 million in public grants on media advertising, and President Carter used more than two-thirds of his allotment for the same purpose.[7] The figures were much the same in 1984. In that year the incumbent, President Reagan, used about 63 percent of his $40.4 million grant on time buys and commercial production, while the challenger, Walter Mondale, devoted 46 percent of his public funding to media.[8] Preliminary estimates for 1988 suggest similar, or slightly increased, media expenditure proportions for both the Democratic and Republican nominees.

Previous Free-time Proposals

The need for free media time has been discussed at least since 1938, when Frank Knox proposed it.[9] Knox had been Republican presidential nominee Alf Landon's running mate in 1936, and his campaign experience convinced him that the escalating costs of *radio* should be reduced with mandatory allocation of free airtime to both parties before each presidential election.

A more recent (1967) and far more detailed proposal was designed by the Twentieth Century Fund Commission on Campaign Costs in the Electronic Era.[10] The commission recommended

> That the federal government provide significant candidates in general election campaigns for President and Vice President of the United States with basic campaign broadcasting access to the American voting public, within the context of programs that will promote rational political discussion and that will be presented in prime evening time simultaneously over every broadcast and cable television facility in the United States.[11]

The commission called the free access "voters' time," and urged that six prime-time thirty-minute programs be made available to each of the two major parties' candidates within thirty-five days of the election (with at least one program broadcast every week.) Third-party candidates were granted lesser amounts of free time (using a method discussed below). Other than simultaneous broadcast over all media outlets, the commission preferred only that the programs "utilize formats that substantially involve the live appearance of the candidates for President and Vice President and are designed to promote rational political discussion for the purpose of clarifying major campaign issues or developing insight into the abilities and personal qualities of the candidates."[12]

The commission did not require that the broadcasters bear the full financial burden of the free media proposal. Rather, the federal government was to subsidize the media outlets at a level of "no more than 50 percent of the commercial 'rate card' charge for such time, or at the lowest charge made to any commercial advertiser for such time, whichever is lower."[13]

In 1978, a Harvard Institute of Politics study group also considered the federal government as the logical if indirect provider of political airtime.[14] Broadcasters would make airtime available to candidates at a discounted rate—but not free—and the stations would then be permitted to deduct from their gross income (for tax purposes) all lost advertising revenue during prime time and two-thirds of their loss during other times.

The Washington-based Center for Responsive Politics recently produced, under a grant from the Markle Foundation, a thorough and thoughtful report on candidates' media access. Among the suggestions was a proposal for free media time that gives great discretion to broadcasters (rather than the political parties), and is also very generous to third-party nominees. The principal recommendations were:

• During every general election period each television station in the nation should be required to provide four half-hour programs on House races during the prime-time access period (7:30–8:00 P.M. weekdays), and four additional half-hours if the market serves a state that has a Senate race. To assure that the presentations have maximum impact, all programs would appear during the four weeks prior to the general election. Time would be equally divided among the major candidates, and all programs would be a half-hour in length.

• While the stations could provide the time to the candidates to use as they wish, they would not have to do so. To permit stations maximum editorial control, and make the time informative to the public, a station could use the time instead for debates or produce other, more innovative formats featuring the candidates.

• To avoid urban candidate glut in House elections, broad-casters could choose the races that receive the free time. The legislation would also specifically authorize stations to discuss among themselves which stations would cover which races, in order to eliminate any concern by broadcasters that such dis-cussions would violate the antitrust laws.

• For both the House and Senate, all candidates whose party obtained at least 5 percent of the vote in the previous election for the same office, or who can obtain petition signatures of 5 percent of the voters in that election, would receive full free-time allocations (that is, time equal to the major parties). Those that receive petition signatures of at least 2 percent would receive allocations amounting to half of the time the major par-ties receive.[15]

A Proposal for "Parties' Time"

The proposal put forth here takes an approach to the free-time question that is quite different from the studies cited above. Spe-cifically, the basic elements of the suggested alternative include:

• *Total Free Time*—As a condition of license renewal, every television and radio station should be required to make avail-able at least eight hours of free time for political advertising every year.

• *Grantees*—The free time should be given not to individual candidates but to the political parties. Each station should an-nually give two hours of time to each of the two major national parties *and* another two hours to each of the state party or-ganizations in the station's primary viewing or listening area (a total of at least eight hours).

• *Free-time Segments*—The time should be granted in 5-minute, 60-second, 30-second, and 10-second spots rather than 30-minute programs. The exact combination of short spots should be left to negotiation between the parties and each me-dia outlet.

• *Guarantees*—Broadcasters must offer a wide variety of time slots, with at least half of the allocations scheduled for weekday evening prime time and at least two-thirds devoted to the September-November period in election years (with most of these spots reserved for the weeks just prior to election day.) Comparable time slots should be made available to each party.

• *Content and Format*—The parties and their candidates should be left completely free to determine the uses to which the free time is put.

• *Remuneration*—There should be no renumeration to broadcasters in any form (public funds, tax credits, and so on) in exchange for the free time.

• *Third Parties*—Lesser parties should be allotted free spots in proportion to the percentage of the vote they received in the prior presidential election (with 5 percent of the vote the minimum threshold necessary to receive any free time.) New parties that did not contest the previous election would receive no free time.

• *Other Advertising Purchases*—Candidates and political parties (major and minor parties) would be free to purchase unlimited additional advertising time at the usual discounted rates.

Discussion of the Proposal's Elements

It is easy to be critical when reviewing the political time policies of America's broadcast industry. No network and virtually no television or radio stations offer any free advertising time to political candidates or parties. Media advertising costs are consuming an increasing portion of all candidates' budgets, and the commercial spot charges have risen far more quickly than the rate of inflation.[16] Yet consider that the public, not the stations, owns the airwaves; airwaves are simply leased for limited durations to the station proprietors. Further, it is not as though station owners cannot afford the sacrifice of a few hours of advertising revenue. American commercial television and radio stations had gross revenues in 1986 of about $27 billion. One industry executive noted recently that commercial television stations are among the most lucrative enterprises in America—their collective profits exceed even that of the oil companies; as he put it, "Having a license to operate a commercial tv station in this country is like receiving the government's permission to print money."[17]

Presently, the United States is the only major democracy in the industrialized world that does not allow the public to reclaim a little of its own airtime for the most vital rituals (elections) and instruments (parties) of democracy.

The sacrifice asked from broadcasters in this free-time proposal is a relatively small one. The vast majority of commercial stations are on the air for at least 6,000 hours per year, and most of them broadcast 1,000 or more hours of advertising annually.[18] A request for eight hours of this time—a tiny fraction of the total—is hardly unreasonable. (In the instances where a station's primary viewing or listening area covers more than one state, or where any third parties qualify for free spots, the free-time request will be slightly greater, but the assertion made here is unchanged.) Because of the flexibility given broadcasters in this plan to schedule the free-time spots, the costs to them will vary considerably from station to station, but in no case can the sacrifice be termed excessive.

There is one aspect of this proposal that is likely to make it more acceptable to broadcasters than some other plans. One of the industry's strongest arguments opposing free-time provisions is that the media markets of many metropolitan stations stretch over a half dozen or more congressional districts, while others incorporate only one or several. A free-time requirement, the broadcasters insist, would unfairly deluge the metropolitan stations with demands that would virtually eliminate all other commercial spots from the air during election seasons. Their claim may be valid if time is given directly to individual candidates,[19] but a free-time grant to state and national *parties* rather than candidates neatly solves the problem, since the vast majority of stations will be accommodating just four (two state and two national party) entities. In this sense, my proposal can be termed a "parties' time" variation of the earlier Twentieth Century Fund Commission's "voters' time."

Generally, we might expect the parties to air institutional advertising in the large media markets—crowding all candidates under the party umbrella without calling special attention to any one. Since 1978 the Republicans have in fact aired spots designed to support the generic party label, and since the 1980 election, the GOP has been using institutional advertising to establish basic election themes. "Vote Republican—for a Change" spots attacked the Democratic Congress in 1980. The then House Speaker Tip

O'Neill was lampooned by an actor who ignored all warning signs and drove a car until it ran out of fuel. ("The Democrats are out of gas," surmised the narrator as Tip futilely kicked the automobile's tire.) Another ad starred a "real-life" unemployed factory worker from Baltimore, a lifelong Democrat who plaintively asked, "If the Democrats are so good for working people, then how come so many people aren't working?"

In the 1982 midterm congressional election the defensive focus of a $15 million GOP institutional campaign was "give the guy [Reagan] a chance" and "stay the course" with the president in the midst of a deep recession and high unemployment. A white-haired mailman was seen delivering Social Security checks fattened with a cost-of-living increase, reminding elderly voters that Reagan had kept his promise, and urging, "for gosh sake, let's give the guy a chance." The spot was highly rated by viewers, like the earlier 1980 ads, and while some moderate Republican candidates resisted being tied to Reagan during one of the most unpopular periods of his presidency, pre- and post-election surveys suggested that the GOP-sponsored media campaign was, on the whole, helpful to individual candidates as well as to the party.[20] The Republicans have also aired generic institutional spots in non-campaign seasons, such as a $1 million series in March 1983 supporting Reagan's economic policies.

While much smaller in scope than the GOP advertising program, the Democrats have also produced a few generic commercials. As early as 1982, the Democrats filmed a series of party spots keyed to the theme "It Isn't Fair—It's Republican."[21] For the 1986 elections, radio ads and one television spot on the farm crisis were aired extensively in nine midwestern states. ("It wasn't just a farm, it was a family. Vote Democratic," intones the narrator as wind whistles through an abandoned barn and farmhouse with the phantom sounds of tractors and mealtime grace fading in and out.)

These "institutional" advertisements are noteworthy innovations in party politics. They permit the party to participate in setting the campaign (or governmental) agenda; they focus on key national themes, thus making politics a bit more comprehensible for the voters while drawing its candidates and officeholders together around common ideas and the party label itself.[22] Survey research on the effects of this kind of advertising demonstrates that it can have a salutary impact on both the party and its nominees: recognition and understanding by the voters of a party's approach and philosophy increases, and (depending on the quality and context of the advertising) substantial gains can be registered for a party's ticket.[23]

The provision of free media time would give both parties the opportunity to make institutional advertising a permanent aspect of the political landscape, and not just at campaign time. Party commercials could be aired during the intervals between campaigns in support of or in opposition to a president's initiatives or policies, or congressional actions (assuming Congress is controlled by one party). State and local parties could also produce institutional advertising for governors, mayors, state legislatures, and city councils.[24]

Despite the generalized advantages of institutional advertising, party leaders should have wide discretion in determining the uses to which the time is put. For instance, in marginal races, they may choose to focus on one or a few specific candidates, and they may prefer to allocate time to nominees for governor or mayor or state legislature, not just for president and Congress. Party officials may conserve most of the airtime for the general election, or may allocate spots to the party's primary or convention candidates to help them become better known before the party nominees are selected.

Whatever the allocation, every candidate would still be free to make whatever additional purchases are necessary and available to promote his or her own individual candidacy. One would hope, however, that substantial free party advertising would reduce the need and demand for individual candidate advertising, thus relieving some of the fund-raising pressure on politicians. This may be a forlorn hope, given competitive campaign realities, but this reform is in any case important because not just the parties but also challengers will so clearly benefit.

Research in political science shows the key financial variable in the competitiveness of congressional elections to be the level of expenditure achieved by *challengers,* not by incumbents.[25] Incumbents are already better known, and thus their expenditures have less additional impact than money spent by relatively unknown challengers. Free media time may increase the competitiveness of our elections by granting greater visibility to challengers, even if it does not result in a significant overall reduction in costs. While both major parties have reason to welcome free exposure, the Democrats would obviously benefit more than Republicans, whose party is generally in a better financial position. (Democrats, for example, are currently able to air only minimal institutional advertising.)

Length, Content, and Format of the Free Time

As noted, free air time should be granted in small segments. A variety of 5-minute, 60-second, 30-second, and 10-second time blocks would compose the eight hours of free time, as opposed to the 30-minute programs preferred by groups such as the Twentieth Century Fund Commission. In an ideal world, where citizens take their responsibilities seriously and care deeply about politics, 30-minute programs might work. But Americans "tune out" pretty quickly when it comes to politics, and channel switching is usually very high for political commercials (or significant political events like debates) that are lengthier than five minutes.[26]

Most voters prefer political advertisements that are short and sweet; any realistic proposal for free media time must take this preference into account. After all, the objective of free time is to facilitate communication between candidates and voters; long political shows merely facilitate the changing of channels and the turning off of sets. The latter option would certainly be exercised by many if not most households if lengthy programs were simulcast, as the Twentieth Century Fund Commission had urged.[27] Given the proliferation of cable systems, simulcasting is no longer a practical option anyway. The only system likely to be acceptable and workable is a flexible one of relatively brief ads.

While not ideal, short ads have advantages beyond the primary one of actually being watched by the public. First, there is the cumulative effect of a series of spot advertisements. Gradually, piece by piece, spots can form a mosaic that projects a candidate's character and platform. They can have the same effect as a feature film of short subjects. Second, a spot advertisement is not more or less truthful than a longer broadcast; it is just as easy for some politicians to lie for thirty minutes as for thirty seconds.

Third, even a very brief commercial can have substantive value. If limited to a single topic, it can reasonably provide an "executive summary" of a politician's point of view. But perhaps most important in terms of the acceptability of this proposal to the broadcast industry, short advertisements provide free political time without significantly disrupting the broadcaster's program schedule. In fact, broadcasters could extract free political time from *programs* (using advanced methods of shortening tapes without obvious effect to the viewer, by eliminating every nth frame,) thus preserving regular paid advertising time.

The precise combination of spot lengths that would compose each party's annual four-hour allocation could be left to negotiation between the parties and individual stations. This is a recognition of the different situations and demands faced by each media outlet, so while standardization of time allocations might make life easier for the parties, this is a reasonable concession to make to broadcasters. Nonetheless, to ensure that the free-time advertisements reach the widest possible audience, the broadcasters should be required to provide a wide variety of time slots, with at least half the allocations scheduled for weekday evening prime time and two-thirds targeted for the September–November period in election years. Given both the rhythm of an election campaign and the tendency of many voters to make their decisions in the final weeks, far more spots should be reserved for late October than early September. A good rule of thumb would be to allocate 10 percent of the general election time for the first half of September, 20 percent for the second half, 30 percent for the first half of October, and the remaining 40 percent for the campaign's last weeks and days. Obviously, the parties should be granted comparable time slots.

The actual content and format of the spots will be determined by the parties (or the individual candidates featured). Many observers and reformers, including the Twentieth Century Fund Commission on Campaign Costs, have suggested mandated personal appearances by the candidates in free time blocks. There is much to recommend this approach: voters may gain more valuable and illuminating insights into the candidates' characters and views when they see them face-to-face (or rather, face-to-screen). Research has indicated that this kind of advertising, termed "talking heads," achieves considerable success with high recall by the audience, however boring or uncreative media consultants believe the format to be.[28] On the other hand, it is naive to think that candidates will not be carefully scripted for live appearances—teleprompters are standard studio equipment today—and video-taped spots can involve dozens of "takes" until the candidate does it just right. Commercial formats without the candidate can also be informative, however, and even animation can be used effectively and educationally by campaigns.[29]

As a rule, neither government nor broadcasters should be able to specify how a candidate or party chooses to appeal to the electorate—in fact, regulating the content and format of political spots is of dubious constitutionality. Parties and candidates should use the media-time grants as they see fit—and to exercise good or bad or even tasteless judgment in so doing. The voters themselves will accept or reject these judgments on election day.

Third Parties and Free Time

No mention has yet been made of third parties. Two-party advocates, such as this author, who believe that the two-party system serves as a bulwark against the fragmentation that often paralyzes countries as diverse as the United States, see nothing wrong in discriminating against third parties when it comes to free media and public financing. The party structure in America helps officeholders aggregate power and mobilize support for their agendas, encourages compromise among competing interest groups under each party's umbrella, assists in making elected officials accountable to their constituents, and presents policy alternatives as well as candidate choices to voters in a manner simple enough to be easily grasped by a frequently distracted public. It is clearly in our country's interest to support and gird the two-party system, which provides such stability and continuity to American democracy, and we would be foolish to encourage fragmentation by providing incentives to third parties. Any scheme of free air time ought to be skewed in favor of the two-party system.

There is ample precedent for such favoritism. For example, in the presidential public funding provisions of the Federal Election Campaign Act (FECA) of 1971, only the White House nominees of the Democratic and Republican parties are awarded a *full* allocation of public money (about $46 million each in 1988) *prior* to the general election campaign. Any third party on the ballot must receive at least 5 percent of the national vote for president, and then—only *after* the election—is entitled to a small allotment in proportion to the vote it garners. On this basis, John Anderson's 7 percent of the vote in the 1980 election entitled him to $4.2 million, paid after November when it could do him relatively little good, compared to the $29.4 million each given to Ronald Reagan and Jimmy Carter. Had Anderson run again in 1984, however, he would have benefited from a provision of FECA that grants a previously successful third party (one that has passed the 5 percent threshold) a sum comparable to what it secured four years earlier, but this time he would have received it before the election. Anderson chose not to exercise his money option in 1984, which would of course have been far less in public funds than Reagan and Mondale received.

Given this precedent, and the benefits of bolstering the two-party system, a free-media plan ought to avoid a "democratic" impulse to grant equal time to third parties. Such access would dramatically increase the time drawn from paid advertising, making broadcasters' cooperation or acquiescence in any free media scheme much less likely.

The Twentieth Century Fund Commission on Campaign Costs in the Electronic Era was relatively generous in its third-party provision for free time. Eligibility for some "voters' time" was extended on a sliding scale to presidential candidates in three categories:

> Category I. Nominees of parties that (a) support the same candidates for President and Vice President in at least three-quarters of the states and qualify electors for those candidates on the ballot in that proportion of states, provided that the electoral votes of these states are sufficient to elect a President and Vice President; *and* (b) ranked first or second in the popular vote in two of the three previous presidential elections. . . .
>
> [Time allocation]: Six prime-time thirty-minute programs within the 35 days preceding the Monday before Election Day, provided that at least one program be broadcast in each seven-day period.
>
> Category II. Nominees of parties that (a) support the same candidates for President and Vice President in at least three-quarters

of the states and qualify electors for those candidates on the ballot in that proportion of states, provided that the electoral votes of these states are sufficient to elect a President and Vice President; *and* (b) received at least one-eighth of the popular vote in the preceding presidential election. . . .

[Time allocation]: Two prime-time thirty-minute programs within the 35 days preceding the Monday before Election Day, provided that no more than one program be broadcast in any seven-day period.

Category III. Nominees of parties that support the same candidates for President and Vice President in at least three-quarters of the states and qualify electors for those candidates on the ballot in that proportion of states, provided that the electoral votes of these states are sufficient to elect a President and Vice President. . . .

[Time allocation]: One prime-time thirty-minute program within the 35 days preceding the Monday before Election Day.[30]

A better and in some ways more restrictive model for third-party time allocation is the FECA public funds provision. Lesser parties should simply be allotted slots based on the percentage of the vote they received in the prior presidential election (with 5 percent the minimum). New parties without electoral track records would have to wait until the next round for free time, providing they passed the threshold. Proportionate free time would be granted to established third parties immediately, a provision that would probably apply initially just to New York, which is the only state with a long and semipermanent tradition of significant third-party organizations (the Liberals and the Conservatives).

Some analysts have suggested that all third parties deserve free media time immediately,[31] based on a polling trigger or number of registered voters' signatures collected, rather than delayed allocation depending on votes previously cast. In practice, these approaches have severe problems, however. Consider allocating free time to third parties on the basis of their passing some threshold figure (for example, 5 or 10 percent support in public opinion surveys). Polls are volatile and imprecise instruments for making such important judgments.[32] A single major event can move survey numbers ten percentage points overnight. And what if a party's trigger percentage fell into a poll's margin-of-error range? What if two usually trustworthy survey organizations differed in their assessments of a third party's strength—one measuring it above the trigger and the other below? For media time allocation in non-presidential races, what should be done in the majority of states that do *not* have regular, reliable surveys of public opinion? And so on.

The other proposal, granting free time to a third party if it can collect the signatures of a percentage of the registered voters (usually 5 percent is suggested) is similarly troublesome. Signatures are *not* the equivalent of votes. Many citizens willingly sign the petitions of candidates they have no intention of supporting. A multitude of high-technology, petition-gathering firms already exist in states with the initiative process to take advantage of the public's predisposition to allow any and all petitioners access to the ballot (or, presumably, access to media time). The appeal to "fairness"—however misleading—is an alluring one for most voters. But free time for all would produce such a glut of requests that the result would more likely be free time for none, since such a system could not survive the inevitable and perhaps justified protests of enraged broadcasters.

Fallback Proposals

In sum, the proposal presented here for free media time has considerable advantages for the political system and is more realistic than most, since it does not require broadcasters to give time to a multitude of candidates and minor parties nor to yield an excessively large block of time. And while directly benefiting strong challengers, the scheme should appeal to incumbents as well, since it does not limit their ability to outpurchase challengers on television and radio while providing supplementary party advertising that might marginally aid the incumbent's reelection in some cases.

Notwithstanding these arguments, however, any such plan is bound to draw substantial opposition. The broadcasting industry fights all proposals for free media time, and the political obstacles preventing enactment of any free-time provision are considerable. Other innovative media plans, such as the already discussed Twentieth Century Fund's *Voters' Time,* have been given short shrift. Off the record, many congressmen express support for the reformer's agenda but don't want to offend district broadcasters whose support or forbearance they perceive as being critical to their re-election. The understandable fear of 535 media-addicted elected officials has landed all previous free-time schemes in the junkyard of good ideas that were legislatively impractical. Any new proposal, however worthy, will obviously face a difficult up-hill struggle.

This fact should not dissuade us from continuing to pursue the free-time idea. In fact, there are new conditions prevailing that might make reform more feasible, such as the manifest, growing concern about the rising level of campaign expenditures (due in good part to the skyrocketing cost of media time) and the failure of other suggested reforms in campaign finance to win approval and reduce the pressure for major change.

To this reformer, at least, it seems clear that a free media man-date ought to be enacted, and without providing any tax credits or other taxpayer-financed subsidies to the broadcast industry. As noted, the public, not the broadcasters, owns the airwaves, and responsible, limited use of this precious resource for the common good appears warranted. Moreover, the industry is an exception-ally wealthy one for which the relatively modest free-time allo-cation would not be a major sacrifice. Reasonable people disagree about this, of course, and given the industry's considerable clout with media-independent politicians, a fallback compromise proposal is prudent.

The fallback position is this: if free time cannot be made avail-able to parties and candidates, then at least the cost of the time ought to be reduced. Currently, thanks to a provision of the Fed-eral Election Campaign Act, broadcasters may only bill candidates for the "lowest unit rate" (l.u.r.) charged their best commercial customers for comparable time. The l.u.r. rule applies only dur-ing the forty-five days preceding a primary election and the six-ty days before a general election. This provision is of singular importance because it establishes in law the principle that expand-ing political communication at an affordable cost takes precedence over broadcasting industry profits.

For a few election cycles, the l.u.r. rule did indeed seem to help, but in the years since the regulation was passed, most television stations have ceased to use "rate cards" with fixed advertising charges.[33] Instead, a virtual auction is held, with time essentially being awarded to the highest bidder. This practice, as well as other changes in how broadcasters sell airtime, has reduced and in many cases nearly eliminated the advantages of the l.u.r. discount for political candidates.[34] For example, the competition and demand for advertising time are much greater today than two decades ago. Discounted spots have always been "preemptible" by full-fare ads, but candidates' commercials faced relatively little threat of being "bumped" in 1971. Today, the danger is so great that the candidates themselves usually opt to pass l.u.r. and pay a higher price for fixed or "nonpreemptible" time. After all, a political spot has often been produced to reach the demographic audience watching television at a particular time, and it will do the candidate little good if the ad is shown at some other time, or worse, not at all.

The Center for Responsive Politics has already suggested an acceptable solution to the discounted advertising problem. The Center proposed redefining l.u.r. to make candidates "preferred preemptible advertisers":

> Candidates buying preemptible time would receive the lowest preemptible rate, and could not be bumped by any other preemptible buy: only an advertiser buying fixed rate time could bump a political advertiser. Since few commercial advertisers buy fixed time, candidates would, in practice, face little danger of preemption if they bought preemptible time under this system. . . .
>
> Because the lowest unit rate today represents a real discount only for preemptible time. . . nonpreemptible time [should] be sold to political candidates at a 30% discount from the average rate charged for that time period over the past year. This would provide candidates with roughly the same discount that lowest unit rate was intended to effect.[35]

To these recommendations might be added two extensions of the l.u.r. or "preferred preemptible advertiser" rule. First, the rule should apply not just to candidates but to the political parties. Parties were not included in the 1971 FECA mandate, and at present they are forced to pay full, undiscounted rates in all circumstances. What is worse, both major political parties have reported great difficulty in getting many stations to sell them time at all, especially during peak, prime-time periods.[36] Second, the rule should apply year-round. Party institutional advertising can rightly be aired continuously, and the legitimate needs of modern campaigns frequently require the airing of early advertising, well before the l.u.r.'s current beginning sixty days prior to the general election (or forty-five days before the primary.)[37] Political communication and voter education are better served by universal calendar application of a discounted rate.

While awaiting congressional action on any sort of discounting or free media time, parties and their candidates should aggressively pursue opportunities for free broadcasts on the nation's 5,500 cable television operations and 800 public access channels.[38] Audience ratings are high for many of these community-based stations, and any channel that can televise live the entire proceeding of the local city council and school board—as up to 2,000 of them apparently do—can obviously afford to make significant amounts of time available to the parties.

Chapter 4
Bolstering the Political Parties

As we have seen, one sure way to lessen the importance of PACs is to shore up competing institutions and to increase the pool of alternative sources of money. To begin with, the $1,000 limit on individual contributions to each candidate per election should be raised to compensate for inflation since 1974. (A $1,000 gift in 1974 is worth less than half that today.) Both the $1,000 cap and the companion limit of $25,000 (maximum total donation to *all* candidates in a calendar year) should be permanently indexed to the inflation rate. If the $25,000 cap were doubled it would merely restore most of its equivalent in 1974 dollars. This adjustment will help offset the financial clout of the PACs.

The Roles of Parties in American Society

Much more vital, however, is the need to enhance the financial flexibility of the political parties. While individuals and PACs represent particular interests, the parties encompass more general concerns. PACs tend to fragment the system; parties push the system toward consensus. In fact, there are no more unappreciated institutions in American life than the two major political parties. Often maligned as the repositories of corrupt bosses and smoke-filled rooms by average citizens as well as by many politicians, the parties nonetheless perform essential electoral functions. Not only do they operate (in part) the machinery for nomination to most public offices, the two parties also help counteract the powerful centrifugal forces in a country teeming with hundreds of identifiable racial, economic, social, religious, and political groups. The parties are often accused of "dividing" us; to the contrary, they assist in uniting us as few other institutions do. They permit elected executives, leaders, and managers to be successful by marshaling citizens around a common standard that can be used to create and implement a public agenda.[1] The enormous good that parties do for American society is indicated by a brief discussion of several of their functions.

Voting and Issue Identification: The political parties provide a useful identification for voters, particularly the least informed and interested, who can use their party affiliation as a shortcut or substitute for interpreting issues and events they may little comprehend. Better-educated and more involved voters also find party identification an assist; few people have time to study every issue or become fully knowledgeable about every candidate seeking public office.

Mobilizing Support and Aggregating Power: The effect of the party identification cue is exceptionally helpful to elected leaders. They can count on virtually automatic support from many of their partisans in times of trouble, for instance. And because there are only two major parties, pragmatic citizens who are interested in politics or public policy are mainly attracted to one or the other standard, creating natural majorities or near-majorities for party officeholders to command. The party creates a community of interest that bonds disparate groups together over time—eliminating the necessity of creating a coalition anew for every campaign or every issue. Imagine the chaos and mad scrambles for public support that would constantly ensue without the continuity provided by the parties. The simplicity of two-party politics may be deceptive, given the vast variety in public policy choices, but a sensible system of representation in the American context might well be impossible without it.

Forces for Stability: As mechanisms for organizing and containing political change, the parties are a potent force for stability. They represent a continuity of approach and attitude in the face of changing issues and personalities, anchoring the electorate as storms are churned by new political people and policies. Because of the unyielding, pragmatic desire to win elections (not just contest them), each party in a sense acts to moderate public opinion.

The party tames its own extreme elements by pulling them toward an ideological center in order to attract a majority of votes on election day.

Governmental Unity, Linkage, and Accountability: Parties provide the glue to hold together the diverse parts of the fragmented American governmental apparatus. The Founding Fathers designed a system that divides and subdivides power, making it possible to preserve individual liberty but difficult to coordinate and produce timely action. Parties help compensate for this drawback by linking the various institutions and loci of power to one another. While rivalry between the executive and legislative branches of American government is inevitable, the partisan affiliations of the leaders of each branch constitute a common basis for cooperation, as any president and his fellow party members in Congress frequently demonstrate. Similarly, the federalist division of national, state, and local governments, while always an invitation to conflict, is more easily coordinated by the intersecting party relationships that exist among officeholders at all office levels. Party affiliation, in other words, is a sanctioned and universally recognized basis for mediation and negotiation—laterally among the branches and vertically among the layers. The party's linkage function does not end there, of course. It helps increase accountability in election campaigns and in government by making candidates and elected leaders account for their performance at party-sponsored forums and in party-nominating primaries and conventions.

Promotion of Civic Virtue and Patriotism: Because identification with a party is at the core of most Americans' political lives, many voters accept and adopt the parties' values and views of responsible citizenship. These values include societal involvement and participation, work for the "public good" in the "national interest" (broadly conceived in partisan terms), and patriotism and respect for American society's fundamental institutions and processes.

The Results of Party Decline

Readers who are unconvinced of the parties' worth after this recitation of their contributions to American society may want to look at the subject from the mirror-opposite perspective. In other words, what would our nation be like without a strong two-party system? Who and what gains as parties decline?

- *Special Interest Groups and PACs Gain.* PAC money, labels, and organizational power can serve as a substitute for the parties' own. Yet instead of focusing on the national interest or a broad coalitional party platform, the candidates' loyalties would be pledged to narrow, special interest agendas instead.
- *Wealthy and Celebrity Candidates Gain.* Individual financial resources or fame can provide name identification to replace party affiliation as a voting identification cue. At least a third of the U.S. Senate seats are currently filled by millionaires, and the number of inexperienced but successful candidates drawn from the entertainment and sports worlds seems to grow each year.
- *Incumbents Gain.* The value of incumbency increases where party labels are absent or less important, since the free exposure that incumbents receive raises their visibility and name recognition. There would also be extra value for candidates endorsed by incumbents or those who run on slates with incumbents.
- *The News Media, Particularly Television News, Gains.* Party affiliation is one of the most powerful checks on the news media, not only because the voting identification cue of the party label is in itself a factor counterbalancing media influence, but also because the "perceptual screen" erected by party identification filters media commentary. (People tend to hear, see, and remember the news items that reinforce their party attitudes and biases.)[2]
- *Political Consultants Gain.* The independent entrepreneurs of campaign technologies (such as polling, political advertising, and direct mail) secure more influence in any system of party decline. They have already become (along with some large PACs), at least to some extent, rivals of the parties, luring candidates from their party moorings and using the campaign technologies to supplant parties as the intermediary between candidates and the voters.[3]

Many thoughtful citizens are deeply troubled by these developments. Most Americans are concerned about the growth of single-issue politics and special interest financing of political campaigns, and most want access to public office to be available to any qualified citizen regardless of wealth or fame. In addition, without the unifying and stabilizing influence of party identification, the news media would gain still further influence, and government conducted through the media is inherently dangerous. Moreover, the personality-cult politics encouraged by television is abhorrent; candidates are unaccountable, aloof from average voters, and prone to stylistic gimmickry. This disturbing trend has been developed by political consultants who hail the medium of television and advance their own interests rather than the parties'. The consultants' main alliance is with incumbent officeholders', whose power they help preserve and who also electorally benefit in some ways from party weakness. With 90 percent or more of incumbent officeholders at all levels regularly reelected, the last trend we ought to encourage is party decline. Vigorous parties help produce competition, which, to judge from the incredibly high incumbent reelection rates, our politics desperately needs.

Despite all of these rationales (both positive and negative) for strong parties, the two-party system in the United States has deteriorated in major ways in the past several decades. For example, fewer voters identify with a political party, and fewer of those who claim an association care intensely about that affiliation.[4] Many social, political, technological, and governmental changes have contributed to party woes. Historically, the government's assumption of important functions previously performed by the parties, such as printing ballots, conducting elections, and providing social welfare services, had a major impact. Particularly in the large cities, party organizations once were a central element of life for millions, sponsoring community events and entertainment, helping new immigrants to settle in, giving food and temporary housing to those in immediate need—all in exchange for votes, of course. But as these social services began to be seen as a right of citizenship rather than a favor extended in exchange for support, and as the flow of immigrants slowed dramatically in the 1920s, party organizations gradually withered in most places.

Simultaneously, the Progressive-inspired direct primary usurped the power of nomination from party leaders and workers, giving it instead to a much broader and more independent electorate and thus loosening the tie between the party nominee and the party organization. Progressive civil service laws also removed much of the patronage used by the parties to reward their loyal followers.

In the post–World War II era, extensive social changes fed the movement away from strong parties. Broad-based education emancipated many voters from complete reliance on identification with the party label. Education also fed the growing issue-oriented politics, which tends to cut across party lines and encourages independent decisionmaking. It also encourages the party-straying habit of ticket splitting. At the same time, millions of people began to move out of the cities, which are easily organized and politicized because of population density, and into the sprawling suburbs, where a sense of privacy and detachment can often deter even the most energetic party organizer. Electorally, as noted, the trends were almost all antiparty: the preeminence of television and the personality politics it brings, the rise of political consultants, the growth of PACs and special interest groups, and the development of a cadre of independent-minded candidates and officeholders who were elected without the help of their parties and wanted to remain as free as possible of party restraints.

Parties and the Campaign Finance Laws

The new campaign finance laws of the 1970s also have had notable effects on the party system. The Federal Election Campaign Act of 1971 was not especially generous to the parties (although neither was it particularly injurious).[5] The 1979 amendments to FECA helped by allowing state and local parties to spend unlimited amounts on materials for volunteer activity and get-out-the-vote drives.[6] The most useful party advantage of all under current law (established in 1978) may be the greatly reduced postage rates allowed party mailings, which are funded by a congressional subsidy.

A thorough discussion of the massive overhaul in campaign finance from 1971 to 1979 is beyond the scope of this report, but it is important to note that the reformers in and out of Congress who spearheaded the changes intended neither to harm the parties nor to strengthen them.[7] In the rush to correct the abuses that surfaced during the Watergate scandals, political parties were often treated as part of the problem, and the parties have had to adapt as best they could to a system not of their own making.

Since then, the parties have overcome many obstacles in the campaign finance statutes and have taken advantage of every opportunity offered by them, expanding and extending the law in ways only dimly foreseen (if at all) by the bills' original backers. For example, in restricting individuals to $20,000 annually in party donations, the new law dried up a valuable source of cash. But the parties responded by initiating broad-based direct-mail programs instead, producing a financial empire of millions of small contributors instead of a relative handful of wealthy contributors. In this way, then, the new law unintentionally benefited the parties.

Another example of the resourcefulness of the parties is found in the provisions regarding contributions to candidates. Party committees are treated in campaign finance law the same as political action committees in one crucial respect: they are limited to direct gifts of $5,000 per candidate per election (with the primary and general election counted separately).[8] But in House races these party contributions are multiplied, since the national party committee, the state party committee, and the national party's congressional campaign committee are usually each eligible to give the $5,000 maximum. Thus, as much as $30,000 ($5,000 × 2 elections [primary and general] × 3 separate party committees) can be directly contributed to every party nominee for the House. In Senate elections, the national party committee and the senatorial campaign committee may give a combined maximum of $17,500 to each candidate, and another $10,000 can be added from the state party committee, for a total of $27,500 in direct gifts.

These contribution limits are not generous, given the enormous costs of competitive election campaigns today. Most Senate candidates, even in small states, spend well over $1 million, and only rarely does a House candidate in a marginal district spend less than a quarter of a million dollars. Fortunately for the parties, direct contributions can be significantly augmented with coordinated expenditures—party-paid general election campaign expenditures (for television advertising, polling, and so on) made in consultation and coordination with the candidate[9] The coordinated expenditure limits are set surprisingly high. In the case of presidential candidates, the national party committees can spend up to two cents for each member of the nation's voting age population (plus an adjustment for inflation)—in 1988 this amounted to about $8.3 million. For House candidates the national and state parties may each spend $10,000, plus an inflation adjustment; the party committees together could thus spend $46,100 in 1988 on behalf of each House nominee.

Senate candidates are the beneficiaries of even higher limits on coordinated expenditures. The national and state parties can each spend $20,000 (plus inflation), or two cents per voter, whichever is greater. In 1988 the party expenditure limits amounted to $92,200 in the eight smallest states, to over $1.9 million in California—or a national total maximum of about $12.8 million for each party in the thirty-three Senate contests. Importantly, the national party committee is permitted to act as the state party committee's spending agent; that is, with the state party's agreement, the national committee can assume the state party's portion of the coordinated expenditures. This privilege centralizes power in the national committees, and unburdens weaker state party committees that otherwise might not be able to contribute the maximum.

Other aspects of the new campaign finance laws have proven far less beneficial to political parties, including the growth of political action committees. Their formation was dramatically spurred by the new campaign laws, and PACs are clearly institutional rivals for the donations of politically active voters as well as the affections of candidate-recipients. Moreover, because of FECA the parties have been especially hamstrung in presidential contests. Since public financing subsidies do not flow through the parties but go directly to presidential candidates, the parties have no role even in certifying candidates for funding eligibility. And since each major-party presidential candidate is limited to an overall general election expenditure ceiling, the limit probably encourages more spending on the "efficient" communication medium of television and less on the barely visible (but possibly more effective) organizational work by the parties.

Pro-Party Reforms

Given the parties' vital centrality in the American system, they should be accorded special, preferential treatment in the statutes that limit and regulate campaign finance. Not only would such reform of the legal structure strengthen the parties directly, it would also indirectly lessen the influence of PACs and interest groups. The current limits on contributions to party committees ($20,000 a year for an individual and $15,000 for a multicandidate PAC) should be substantially increased. Individuals as well as corporations, labor unions, and trade associations should be permitted to underwrite all administrative, legal, and accounting costs parties incur, with full disclosure of all donations but without limiting the amount of those donations.

Even more important would be the enactment of a tax credit to benefit the parties. Before landmark tax reform legislation was passed in 1986, federal taxpayers were granted a 50 percent tax credit for all contributions to candidates, PACs, parties, and political committees, of up to $50 for an individual and $100 on a joint return. Unfortunately this credit was eliminated in the 1986 tax revision, allowing no deduction for political gifts. The credit, this time applying only to parties, ought to be reestablished at least to the 50 percent level, and if possible all the way to 100 percent. Such a move would clearly encourage small donations that have few if any real strings attached; the parties would not only remain unencumbered by the perceived obligations that come with large contributions, but both parties would have an exceptionally valuable tool to use in expanding their donor and membership base.[10] This would be especially effective if forty-three income-taxing states agreed to match the 50 percent credit of the federal government, if that were the federal limit; taxpayers in these states would, then, in effect get a 100 percent credit.[11]

Realistically, in an era when gigantic budget deficits threaten even existing programs, the prospects of securing a new credit at the federal level, or at the state level in any but a few of the wealthier states, do not appear promising. Similarly, grandiose schemes for full public financing of either parties or candidates are unlikely to win passage. There is considerable evidence of substantial public hostility to providing public officials with taxpayer-funded reelection treasuries to supplement their generous taxpayer-financed salaries and perquisites.[12] Beyond that, campaign financing is simply not a high priority for most voters who are concerned about economic conditions, health care, and other more immediate matters. In one survey, a series of spending alternatives was posed to respondents, forcing them to make the same choices often faced by policymakers.[13] Everything—from bridge repairs and missile defense systems to health care and budget balancing—was rated far more important than public financing of political campaigns. Moreover, when respondents were asked whether they would favor or oppose "giving people a full tax credit for contributing money to a political party," a solid majority of 55 percent was opposed (39 percent were in favor, 5 percent had no opinion.)[14] This is somewhat surprising, since the public is usually inclined to approve tax credits that might provide some benefit to it. Respondents' negative reactions might signify concern about the budget deficit or, more likely, estrangement from political parties.

There is, however, another option that could win both public and legislative favor: a tax "add-on" that would permit a citizen to channel up to $100 of his income tax refund to the party of his or her choice. Both parties would clearly gain funds, but the budget deficit would be none the worse for it. The voluntary nature of this self-imposed tax would appeal to conservative and Republican citizens, while the ready cash would draw the assent of money-starved Democratic and Liberal party activists. In its ideal form, the federal 1040 (short and long form) and every annual income tax form on the state level should include an add-on provision that gives a taxpayer the opportunity to check off a gift of $2, $5, $10, $25, $50, or $100 to the party he or she designates.

Will taxpayers actually give money through this add-on option? Five states (California, Maine, Massachusetts, Montana, and Virginia) currently have some form of add-on. The Virginia experience has been that about 2.2 percent of all eligible taxpayers have made contributions, yet even this tiny portion has provided several hundred thousand dollars cumulatively to the parties. Participation rates in other states have been somewhat higher, averaging about 4 percent.[15] While giving even small amounts to the political parties will doubtless never become the rage among beleaguered taxpayers anticipating a refund, it is likely that the present minuscule percentage of participation could be substantially augmented by a joint two-party educational advertising campaign undertaken at tax time. The campaign might profitably be keyed to patriotic themes, urging citizens to demonstrate their civic commitment in this small but critical way. The parties would be wise to take full advantage of this golden entry on the tax forms, if it is enacted, and they should encourage the add-on option in all states where it does not now exist.

It ought to be mentioned here that the universe of potential contributors to the parties, while not enormous, is often underestimated. As the Republican and Democratic National Committees have demonstrated with direct mail, millions of Americans are willing to give them small- and medium-size amounts of money if the right stimulus is applied. In one 1986 survey, nearly half of the respondents (48 percent) indicated they had contributed money at least once to a political campaign, and 19 percent of these contributors claimed to have donated more than $100 in a single year.[16] Undoubtedly there is some "good citizen" overreporting in these figures, or perhaps some are counting their $1 checkoff to the presidential Federal Election Campaign Fund on the 1040 form, but even factoring in those considerations there is a surprisingly substantial total. In any given year, of course, the proportion of people making a contribution is much less; during presidential years, it has been measured at between 8 and 13.5 percent, with only about 4 percent giving to the parties rather than (or as well as) individual candidates or PACs.[17] The more parties can develop closer personal contact with their partisans, and the more they can leverage the funding options at their disposal, the higher will be their yield. The potential is great for cultivating grass-roots loyalty. An "add-on" provision—possibly the only campaign finance reform to which no one can have serious objection and thus the most feasible proposal on the table—would be one way for parties to fulfill their financial potential.

Fortunately for those who see the compelling need for stronger parties, progress and realization are already under way on many fronts. There are winds at the parties' backs today, forces that are helping to reverse decades of decline. None may be more important than the growing realization of the worth of political parties by many journalists and officeholders, as well as the continued advocacy of party-building reforms by many academics and political practitioners. The resolve of recent national party leaders to strengthen their organizations—such as past Republican National Committee chairmen William Brock and Frank Fahrenkopf and Democratic party leaders Paul Kirk (former Democratic National Committee chairman) and Tony Coelho (chairman until 1987 of the Democratic Congressional Campaign Committee)—has been of paramount significance to the ongoing revival of political party organizational and financial might.

As noted earlier, the national and state parties have been newly aggressive and shrewdly creative in exploiting the opportunities currently available to them under existing campaign finance laws. Despite the decline in voter affiliation with the parties, then, there is still reason for optimism regarding the ability of the party organizations to make full use of the advantageous changes in the law advocated here, should they be enacted.

The Political Parties and Public Financing

President Theodore Roosevelt first proposed in 1907 that the cost of campaigns be borne by the federal Treasury: since 1976, as a result of the Watergate scandals, presidential campaigns have been publicly financed, but congressional races have not been. Three major attempts in the late 1970s and two tries in the 1980s to extend the presidential system to Congress failed.[18]

Despite public financing's unpopularity, one day a Democratic Congress and a Democratic president may enact and sign a bill establishing publicly funded congressional elections. Solid Democratic control does not guarantee it however; President Carter and the heavily Democratic Congress of his term failed to enact public financing in the late 1970s. But Democratic control is probably a precondition of reform, given the nearly solid conservative GOP opposition and the current Republican fund-raising edge that would be partially neutralized if public funding were to take effect. If it did, taxpayer dollars should be channeled through the state parties, with some reasonable proportion of the funds (perhaps 10 to 20 percent) retained by the parties for their own administrative expenses and party-building tasks.[19] For instance, the party might want to spend the public money by undertaking a voter contact (canvassing) program that would strengthen the party's base while benefiting all party candidates. A get-out-the-vote effort on election day would be another sensible application of funds.

From the standpoint of the party, it would also be advantageous if parties were given some discretion in allocating the public monies to their congressional candidates. Obviously, safe incumbents in one-party districts need far less support than candidates in two-party marginal districts. Every party candidate should be guaranteed a minimum amount, but the parties should have the authority to concentrate resources where they can do the most good. It is difficult to imagine, however, that incumbent members of Congress—who would pass any public financing plan—would ever permit parties to exercise this degree of discretion. After all, the parties conceivably could use this power to discipline a recalcitrant lawmaker by withholding funds. And, since this extra increment of cash would be far more useful to the generally poorer Democrats than to the well-heeled Republicans, most GOP legislators are likely to be unreceptive to the idea.

There are real risks for both parties in public financing schemes, since it is highly likely that Congress will choose to bypass them entirely, giving the money directly to candidates (as it did with public financing at the presidential level). Thus, infused with a new source of money not connected to the parties, nominees will be even more independent of their parties than they are now; moreover, the parties will receive no financial bonus to promote their own programs. At the other extreme, if the parties were generously funded, it is possible that some state parties would lazily permit themselves to become overly dependent on an effortless source of funds, allowing their own grass-roots fund-raising apparatus to atrophy. There have been occasional reports of this distressing phenomenon at the state level when public subsidies were provided to the parties.[20]

On the whole, though, the states' experiences in public financing offer some hope.[21] Twenty-one states have established public financing schemes, and slightly more than half funnel the money through the parties.[22] Almost all of the public-finance states that utilize the parties as conduits allow them to use portions for their own administrative expenses. In North Carolina, for example, about one-quarter of the operating revenue of both major parties is provided by public funds, and in a number of states the money has been well spent by parties on in-kind services to candidates modeled after the national parties' successful programs.[23] Iowa gives its parties more leeway than perhaps any other state, with the state central committees permitted to spend funds for any legitimate campaign purpose, from media advertising to staff salaries and expenses for candidates and their aides. Further, Iowa and a majority of the party-financing states allow the state central committees at least some discretion in distributing tax dollars to their nominees—an arrangement that magnifies the influence that party leaders can exert over their candidates.

Any public financing scheme at the federal level would certainly do well to follow the example set by some of the states. The Congress could make a useful start by providing the national parties with an untapped source of revenue requiring no enlargement of the deficit or new taxes. The Federal Election Campaign Fund—the repository for contributions from the federal $1 income-tax check-off—annually receives somewhere between $30 million and $40 million.[24] The only major disbursements are to qualifying presidential candidates and the parties to pay for their presidential nominating conventions, and this regularly leaves the fund with a sizable surplus. Even after the bills from the 1984 presidential contest were paid, there was a surplus of almost $93 million.[25] (Just a year later, at the end of 1985, the surplus had grown to almost $126 million.)[26] It would not greatly tax the fund if $5 million per election cycle were provided to each of the national party committees to use for party-building purposes and administrative expenses.

The relative poverty of the Democrats' treasury actually stands in the way of some substantial pro-party reforms. For example, why should the GOP agree to initiate public financing when the party is already well funded under existing rules and any such change may well benefit the Democrats disproportionately? Conversely, the Democrats will block any increase in the amount parties can give to their congressional candidates, since only the Republicans could afford to give above the current maximums. Still Republican National Committee Chairman Frank Fahrenkopf is surely correct in wondering "why the United Auto Workers or NCPAC [National Conservative Political Action Committee] can spend an unlimited amount of money supporting or opposing candidates for federal office [by means of independent expenditures] and not the Republican or Democratic parties."[27] At some point in the future the amounts party committees can give or spend on behalf of their nominees should be considerably increased, but not until the Democratic party is better funded and there is a more reasonable balance in resources between the two major parties. Many desirable pro-party changes in the campaign finance law may have to be deferred until then. But the long-term objective is clear: beef up the parties so that PACs will be limited *indirectly*. Candidates and the political system will benefit from the infusion of more party funds and influence, while PACs will remain free from cumbersome restrictions.

Chapter 5
Other Reform Ideas That Do Some Good

Public Funding and Tax Credits

If and when public financing is passed, it may not be designed in ways that benefit the parties. Consequently an alternate public financing scheme could be tailored to benefit the political system in other ways, such as increasing (not reducing) competition. Accordingly, if public funds are given directly to candidates, they ought to be granted as an expenditure *floor* rather than a *ceiling*.

Under this plan, every congressional candidate who can qualify by raising a certain amount (say, $50,000) in small contributions (perhaps $250 and under) will be eligible for matching funds from the federal Treasury for all similar small gifts, up to an agreed public-funds maximum per candidate of perhaps $50–75,000. In the general election each congressional nominee of a major party would receive a certain flat amount (a floor) in public funds (perhaps $150,000) to ensure that he or she reached the minimum financial threshold necessary to conduct a modern, high-tech campaign. (A third-party candidate should receive a share of this "floor" funding level *after* the general election, in proportion to the vote he or she has received over a minimum 5 percent level, similar to the current arrangement for presidential candidates.)

Beyond the public grants, each candidate in both the primary and general elections should be permitted to raise as much as possible in unrestricted fashion from PACs and from individuals. This approach guarantees at least a degree of competition in each district by enabling all qualified candidates to communicate with voters while preserving for individuals, PACs, and interest groups a rightful and legitimate role in elections.

A ceiling on expenditures, on the other hand, almost certainly minimizes competition and benefits incumbents, since challengers must usually spend a great deal more than officeholders to defeat them. Moreover, a ceiling restricts the flow of communications between candidates and voters, unfairly minimizes the direct participation of PACs in the political process, and squeezes PAC money into less accountable and less desirable channels, such as independent spending.

Realistically, these reform measures do not have a good chance of enactment. Congressmen are probably not going to do any favors for their opponents by enacting public-funding floors that favor challengers rather than ceilings that favor themselves. Representative Richard Cheney (R–Wyo.) said it best: "If you think this Congress, or any other, is going to set up a system where someone can run against them on equal terms at government expense, you're smoking something you can't buy at the corner drugstore."[1] Cheney's observation is a warning that applies to the whole of the campaign-finance reform agenda, for when all is said and done, it is Congress—not PACs or campaign-finance academics or public interest lobbyists—that passes revisions in campaign laws. And Congress is certain to take care of its own. In the field of political money, the best advice remains *Caveat reformator:* Let the reformer beware.

Probably the best form of public financing with a reasonable chance of passage is the tax credit option. I have argued in favor of restoring the pre–1986, 50 percent tax credit for all contributions to political parties up to $50 for an individual and $100 on a joint return. A useful and feasible companion reform would be to restore the old credit for small gifts to House and Senate candidates, too. Gifts to PACs, which were included in the tax credit formerly available, should continue to be excluded from such eligibility. The political activities of PACs and interest groups should not be subsidized by the taxpayers.

Reforming the tax credit option would slightly diminish the incentive to give to PACs and increase the motivation for party and candidate giving. And while challengers would benefit from a form of public financing that increases the electoral money supply without capping expenditure, incumbents would perhaps be in a better position to take advantage of the small-donor tax credit because of their superior resources and higher name recognition. Not incidentally, recent elections have underlined the need to stimulate more small, individual contributions. Gifts of under $100 to House candidates have declined from 38 percent of all campaign money in 1978, to 22 percent in 1982, and 20 percent in 1984.[2]

Increasing the tax credit for small gifts would encourage greater citizen participation while providing another indirect check on PACs. It might also help stem another unhealthy development, the accumulation of large personal debts by candidates (especially nonincumbents) during their campaigns. In 1984, for instance, 12 percent of all funds secured by House candidates were in the form of loans by the candidates themselves from their personal fortunes or from bank lending. These loans can place elected representatives in a suspect position once in office, as they attempt to repay the banks (or themselves) with either PAC money or individual contributions.[3] While fund-raising pressure is a constant for all congressmen whether they have debts or not, personally secured loans are particularly worrisome, since they present the opportunity for the lending banks to assert undue influence (although they are strictly regulated on this score). Or, in the case of a loan from a candidate's personal monies, postelection PAC and individual gifts can go right into a congressman's pocket as he repays the loan to himself.

Disclosure: The Best Reform

Probably the most universally supported and certainly the most successful provision of the campaign finance law is disclosure, whereby PACs and candidates are required at various intervals to reveal their contributions and contributors as well as their expenditures. Not only do the disclosure provisions expose the motives and decisions of PACs and politicians, they also alert competing interests to the need for mobilization. Disclosure is no cure-all, however. As political scientist David Adamany has pointed out, the disclosure laws generate more information than can be mastered by the media or the voters.[4] The volume of financial disclosure reports filed with the Federal Election Commission is crushing. The FEC does an admirable job in making this information available to press and public, despite inadequate funding, but it is usually well after election day before any thorough analysis of the data can begin—too late to affect the election results. Still, disclosure serves many useful purposes, from permitting postelection enforcement of the laws to allowing comparisons to be made between campaign contributions and votes cast on the floor of Congress. Disclosure itself generates pressure for more reform. When campaign finance was out of sight, it was out of most people's minds; now that the trail of money can be more easily followed, indignation is only a press release away.

There are many recent examples of the salutary effects of disclosure, but one will suffice to prove the point. Shortly after becoming chairman of the Senate Finance Committee in January 1987, Senator Lloyd Bentsen (D–Tex.), a vice presidential candidate in 1988, offered about two hundred Washington lobbyists and political action committee directors the opportunity to have breakfast with him once a month for the price of a $10,000 contribution to his reelection campaign. Following press disclosure of his "Chairman's Council" and a torrent of adverse publicity about these "Eggs McBentsen" breakfasts, the senator dissolved the club and returned the money.[5] Five other senators with similar fundraising organizations refused to follow suit but now conduct their activities under the increased scrutiny of press, public, and, most importantly, their present and future political opponents.[6] This potential electoral vulnerability has helped to inhibit the actions of congressmen.

Disclosure enables voters to take advantage of the very Achilles' heel that large contributors attempt to leverage: the incumbent's perpetual political insecurity—an insecurity that affects even congressmen from supposedly "safe" districts. As argued earlier, votes matter more than campaign money, and, whenever potential donations threaten electoral security, the choice between the two is an easy one for most politicians. Accordingly, since disclosure is a powerful check against abuses that even tightly drawn laws cannot always prevent or foresee, it makes sense to establish broad, timely, and complete disclosure of all political money.

Disclosure, then, is the single greatest check on the excesses of campaign finance, for it encourages corrective action, whether by the politicians themselves, by the judiciary through prosecution in the courts, or by the voters at the polls. It is such an essential and welcome device in American democracy that it should be broadened to bring to light a number of abuses or perceived abuses in the PAC and political party community. No PAC practice is so distasteful as the distortion and deception found in many direct-mail solicitations, especially from the ideological committees. PACs using any form of direct-mail fund-raising should be required to enclose a copy of all letters with their periodic FEC reports.

Successful direct-mail fund-raising often uses some of the same tactics as advertising, including exaggeration and deceptive promises.[7] Journalist Robert Timberg of the *Baltimore Sun* documented a number of such cases in a newspaper series on PACs.[8] An anti-abortion group calling itself "Stop the Baby Killers" promised in 1979 to give maximum contributions to candidates opposing a number of "Political Baby Killers" (liberal Democratic congressmen), and to pay for polls, in-kind campaign consultants, and campaign training seminars for volunteers. In truth, the group made not a single contribution of any size to a candidate in 1979 or 1980, conducted no polls, and held no campaign seminars. What happened to the $189,000 the group raised? About $146,000 was used to pay three for-profit direct-mail firms with ties to the organization itself.

Another disturbing example occurred when less than 3 percent of the nearly $1.7 million Congressman Edward Markey's two PACs (the U.S. Committee Against Nuclear War and the National Committee for Peace in Central America) raised from 1982 to 1986 was contributed to candidates sympathetic to the Massachusetts Democrat's causes. His PACs broke repeated promises to 50,000 contributors that their money would be used to train and elect liberal contenders, lobby legislators, and conduct polling, canvassing, and phone banks.[9] The FEC has received many complaints about fraudulent political fund-raising, and this may be only the tip of the iceberg. Unless a reporter happens to receive a copy of a questionable solicitation or a contributor takes it upon himself to trace his money through the FEC, little is heard about most direct-mail pieces. PACs using direct mail should be required to disclose (in each letter and on each contributor card) how much of all money raised is devoted to fund-raising and administrative costs. The recipients may not like what they read and consequently may refuse to give, but they are entitled to know how their money will be spent if any degree of accountability is to exist. Furthermore, *all* PACs, not just those using direct mail, should be required to report their list of candidate selections to their contributors. Most PACs already do this, but the ideological PACs, which frequently use direct mail and are far removed from their donors, are usually exceptions.

Beyond mandating further accountability by PACs, fuller disclosure is needed in other areas as well. Both national parties have a "building fund," for example, to pay the costs of the headquarters' facilities; corporations, unions, and individuals have contributed millions of dollars to these funds, which, for the most part, have remained hidden from public view.[10] Large contributors are given their weight in golden access to party officeholders. At the 1988 Democratic National Convention, for instance, donors of $200,000 or more to the Democratic National Committee were entitled to twenty seats at the convention, the use of plush skyboxes, and sessions with the party's star attractions, including the presidential nominee.[11] (It should be noted here that $200,000 is *forty* times the maximum donation allowed per election by a political action committee to any federal candidate.) The Republican party gave similar status and access to large contributors at its summer convention.[12]

Finally, some presidential candidates (as well as some large PACs) have established tax-exempt foundations that do little else than prepare the groundwork for their sponsors' White House bids. Yet these foundations can accept unlimited donations from groups and individuals and do not have to disclose the identities of any donors.[13] Some potential candidates have voluntarily revealed their foundations' benefactors, but they should not have the option not to reveal them. And the perpetually starved Federal Election Commission must be funded at a much more generous level to accommodate the increased crush of paper that comes with broadened disclosure.[14]

Soft Money

Another area where the disclosure laws need considerable expansion is "soft money." This term refers to political contributions that would be illegal under federal law but are acceptable under the laws of certain states. For example, individual gifts over $1,000 per election as well as direct contributions from corporate and union treasuries are prohibited by FECA, yet are permitted in most states. As long as the money is channeled through state political parties for "party-building" activities (voter registration drives, get-out-the-vote efforts, and the like) and not tied directly to the election of federal candidates, essentially unlimited sums can be spent. In many states with loose reporting requirements, allocation of the money is largely undisclosed to the state elections board and for the most part is not reportable to the Federal Election Commission.[15]

Unquestionably, soft money affects federal elections. How could it be otherwise, when the parties use it to register thousands of voters and ensure that they get to the polls on election day? Any suggestion to the contrary ignores political realities. On the other hand, the same money is clearly and simultaneously affecting state and local races, which are totally independent of federal election law; every ballot, after all, lists contests for state and local offices as well as national ones.

Thus, it is practically impossible to separate soft-money expenditures for federal campaigns from those for nonfederal candidates, and given overlapping state and federal jurisdictions, it would be difficult and even unfair to try to enforce the stricter federal contribution limits. But surely it is not too much to ask that *all* campaign contributions affecting federal contests be disclosed *in full*. Such a requirement ought to be based on the fundamental principle that *hidden* money is *dangerous* money in democratic elections.

This is not a trivial problem. While no hard and fast calculations are possible, an estimated $15 to 20 million was raised and spent on soft money during the 1984 presidential election by both parties.[16] In 1988 the collection of soft money became a high priority for both presidential campaigns. The Democrats raised in excess of $20 million from federally prohibited sources, and the Republicans did at least as well. Actually, it is possible that much more soft money was secured by the two parties, but these are the threshold amounts to which party officials will admit. Even if $40 million is accepted as the two-party combined total, soft-money expenditures thereby increased well over 100 percent in just four years.[17]

From where are these very large contributions coming? The answer is obvious: labor unions, corporations, and individuals who feel too restrained by the current federal limits. Their collective influence can be worrisome, as the Center for Responsive Politics demonstrated in a study of soft-money gifts in five states during 1985–86. About $3.3 million was given to state parties just in California, Colorado, Florida, Missouri, and Washington over one election cycle. A single contributor gave $100,000 to the Florida GOP and $85,000 to the California Democrats; perhaps coincidentally, a U.S. senator subsequently interceded on behalf of this generous donor with federal regulators in 1987, an action that potentially saved the financier millions of dollars as a result.[18]

The Honoraria Problem

Those who fear the vote-buying potential of PAC money might better direct their attention to the $9.8 million awarded in 1987 by interest groups directly to legislators, not as campaign contributors but as "speaking fees" and honoraria.[19] This 1987 sum represented more than a 400 percent increase over the 1984 total.[20] While PAC and other campaign contributions are devoted to the legitimate public purpose of democratic elections, honoraria are placed directly in the private pockets of lawmakers.

Not surprisingly, the most powerful and influential congressmen receive the largest fees.[21] For example, in 1987, eighteen of the Senate's highest earners were either in leadership posts, on the Senate Finance Committee, committee chairmen, or ranking minority members.[22]

These congressmen often needed only to make a brief appearance at a breakfast seminar or executive luncheon; under rules the legislators themselves devised, members of Congress can accept up to $2,000 per appearance; House members can take up to 30 percent of their annual salary in honoraria (or $26,850 in 1988) and senators are allowed 40 percent (or $35,800 in 1988).

Yet congressmen can actually accept any amount as long as cash over the "limits" is donated to "charities" of the legislator's choice. As Common Cause has noted, congressional rules do not require the disclosure of the identity of the charities, nor do most congressmen release their tax returns. Thus, it cannot be determined whether they are taking the charitable deduction for these gifts—

which, after all, would be the equivalent of money in their pockets. The charities selected are normally in the home state or district, with the gifts frequently generating positive publicity for the congressman and strengthening his or her electoral position at home.

The unappealing, suspect nature of honoraria fees was starkly illustrated in 1987 when several key congressmen were paid $2,000 each at a breakfast briefing by a truck manufacturer just before a House Armed Services subcommittee hearing where the manufacturer won an extension on its $239 million annual government contract.[23] Even the company vice president—when the incident was uncovered more than a year later—sheepishly admitted, "It looks kind of funny, doesn't it?" But one of the congressmen who took the cash and apparently voted the company's way on a voice vote had a different reaction: "I guarantee you, if they call me again and say, 'Would you like to come up here and get an honorarium?' I'll do it. You can take that to the bank."[24]

Even more disturbing may be the latest enticement interest groups are offering legislators: all-expense paid trips to resorts around the nation and the world for congressmen and, sometimes, family members.[25] The sponsoring groups reimburse the congressmen for travel expenses incurred in connection with their speaking engagements at vacation centers—often in addition to the regular honorarium fee. In other words, business trips are converted to luxury family vacations paid for by special interests. The practice is becoming common. Between 1980 and 1985, Common Cause found that the average number of travel reimbursements claimed by senators increased by about 20 percent and that the number of nights they spent away on the tab of interest groups rose by over 50 percent. For House members, the gains were much larger: reimbursements more than doubled, and nights spent away more than tripled.[26] Not surprisingly, most if not all of this travel is perfectly permissible under the lax ethics rules of the House and Senate.[27]

PAC contributions receive most of the media attention, but honoraria and free trips ought to be the focus of those worried about undue influence and corruption in the legislative branch. Congress ought to restrict or eliminate honoraria and special interest junketing; it should not tolerate even implied corruption.

While these fees and trips are often excused as necessary income supplements for a Congress that will not pay its members the substantial salaries they deserve, this is not the way to remedy that insufficiency.

The Congressional Golden Parachute

There is much for reformers to attack in the field of campaign finance, but the most strident outrage may be a little-noted "grandfather" clause in federal election law permitting any member of Congress who was in office on January 8, 1980, to keep any remaining campaign contributions for *personal* use after leaving office.[28] As part of the 1979 amendments to the Federal Election Campaign Act, Congress barred the conversion of the excess campaign funds to personal use. But the current members were exempted (or grandfathered) at the insistence of the House. (Internal Senate rules prohibit members from using campaign money for personal purpose, yet once a member leaves the Senate, internal rules can no longer be enforced.)

Some retiring members have been ethical enough to return accumulated campaign cash to their donors or to give it to charities or political party committees. (The amounts involved are not minuscule; grandfathered members of Congress collectively held $42 million in their 1987 war chests—an average of almost $200,000 each.) But many have not been shy about converting cash given for their reelection races into supplementary pensions or personal slush funds.[29] One former House member purchased a new Cadillac as a "going away" gift to himself; others have bought everything from furniture to flowers, with interest-free loans being particularly popular.[30] Most, however, have simply pocketed the money. "I will use it to help tide me over," said one, while another only "wished it had been more."[31] Of the sixty-five representatives who possessed surpluses of $300,000 or more, fifty-one used their golden parachute to land safely and securely in retirement.[32]

U.S. Representative Andrew Jacobs (D–Ind.), although grandfathered, has sought to abolish the loophole. Explained Jacobs: "These funds are given for a *purpose*—to get elected—not to provide a civil service retirement fund. We already have a generous one. When I think of those who have engaged in this sort of practice, only the word 'sleazy' comes to mind."[33] Surely this clause deserves to be repealed—with excess campaign funds returned *pro rata* to contributors or donated to charity (without congressmen receiving the charitable tax deduction).[34] Of course, repeal of this provision will not come easily, since 191 of the current membership of the House are beneficiaries of it. Most congressional leaders are among the grandfathered representatives.

Still, Congress came tantalizingly close to responsible reform in early 1989, when the grandfather clause, as well as the pocketing of honoraria, was slated for banning in exchange for a substantial (51 percent) salary increase. Regrettably, the reforms were torpedoed when the pay hike succumbed to popular protest. Yet the grandfather clause is so abominable it deserves to be repealed even without a pay supplement.

The Impasse on Independent Expenditures

The independent PACs operate outside of [the] framework of accountability and simply become hit artists on the political scene.
— Senator Paul Sarbanes (D–Md.)[35]

I'm against independent expenditures. I do not think they help the political process . . . because they decrease accountability. . . . I think candidates should be accountable for charges that are brought up. . . .
— John "Terry" Dolan, former chair of the National Conservative Political Action Committee (NCPAC)[36]

It is not easy for a liberal Democratic senator who was a prime NCPAC target in his 1982 reelection race and the former chairman of NCPAC to find common ground, but the issue of accountability in independent spending is apparently an area on which they agree. An independent expenditure is money spent by an individual or a group to support or defeat a candidate; the expenditure is made *without consultation with, or the cooperation of, any candidate or campaign.* Thus, voters cannot hold candidates accountable for charges made against their opponents by an independent group. In addition, since there are *no limits* on the amount of independent expenditure money that can be spent, it undermines a basic intent of the campaign laws.[37] The frequent use of negative, even vicious, messages and tactics by independent groups makes any sort of civility in politics much more difficult to achieve. And the groups' minimal contact with their contributors—since most of their cash is raised by direct mail—leaves them unaccountable to their own donors in addition to the voters at large.

Despite these widely acknowledged difficulties, and the opposition to unlimited independent expenditures by political figures as diverse as former Senator Barry Goldwater (R–Ariz.) and former Senator George McGovern (D–S. Dak.), every attempt to rein in the independent groups has so far failed. One unsuccessful try was made by the Federal Election Commission to enforce a key provision of the Presidential Campaign Fund Act that bars PACs from spending more than $1,000 each on behalf of a presidential nominee who has accepted public financing.[38] The proximate cause of the failure was the Supreme Court's 1976 decision in *Buckley v. Valeo.*[39] The Court held that PACs and individuals, acting completely on their own, could advocate a candidate's election or defeat without limit. But the real obstacle to this reform is the First Amendment to the U.S. Constitution guaranteeing free speech, on which the *Buckley* decision was based. So precious is this right that, however noxious the independent groups' spending may be, it would be a dangerous and blatantly unconstitutional error to stifle it.

Even though independent spending itself should not be restricted, its negative effects can be somewhat tempered by boosting its political rivals. Thus, it would be useful to strengthen the financial role of the political parties in elections, as well as to increase the pool of small individual givers through tax credits. It would also be helpful to provide free media time, an initiative that would indirectly help reduce the importance of independent spending. Beyond that, requiring the disclosure of direct-mail letters, candidate selections, and organizational fund-raising costs (as proposed earlier) might also take the wind out of the sails of some independent expenditure groups.

Several reform bills have been introduced in Congress to provide candidates with free response time when they are attacked or when their opponent is supported by independent groups. For example, several legislators have championed provisions awarding an aggrieved candidate either free radio and television advertising (courtesy of broadcasters) or a grant from public funds equal to the amount of the independent expenditure whenever independent spending against him or her tops $5,000.[40] However, the former proposal may be of questionable constitutionality because it in effect discourages broadcasters from accepting independent ads by forcing them to provide equal response time free of charge. And the latter proposal overlooks the ingenuity, inventiveness, and the aggressiveness of the independent groups. NCPAC actually welcomed the idea, announcing that it would simply run $100,000 in ads "attacking" a favored candidate and urging that he or she be defeated for "lowering taxes, opposing busing, and standing for a strong defense." Besides identifying its candidate with a litany of popular positions, NCPAC's independent salvo would trigger another $100,000 in free time for him or her.

"We don't have a perfect solution," admits Common Cause's Fred Wertheimer, who has backed some of the reform proposals, "There's always going to be a problem with independent expenditures."[41] Perhaps the fact that many independent groups are financially floundering and that their spending campaigns failed or even backfired in 1984 and 1986 will serve as some consolation to those who have unsuccessfully tried to reform this constitutionally valid but vexing phenomenon.[42]

Conclusion

This agenda for constructive reform of the American system of campaign finance targets real and quasi corruption and rejects the reform of pseudo corruption; it requires the avoidance of harmful remedies as well as the enactment of helpful measures. Changes to be avoided include:

- the artificial elimination of political action committees or enactment of unworkable limitations on their campaign contributions;
- the establishment of artificial and inflexible expenditure ceilings;
- a ban on nonresident contributions to congressional candidates.

Changes to be encouraged include:

- free television and radio time for candidates and parties;
- a 50 or 100 percent tax credit for small donations to parties and candidates;
- an income tax refund "add-on" provision for political parties and an annual party subsidy from the surplus in the Federal Election Campaign Fund;
- a doubling of the current individual contribution limits and a substantial rise in individual and PAC gift limits to the parties, with permanent inflation indexing for all limits;
- broadened disclosure to expose all potentially dangerous hidden political money (such as soft money, donations to party-building funds, and presidential candidates' tax-exempt foundations);
- PAC abandonment of the practice of giving to opposing candidates, and a moratorium on donations to previously opposed candidates until at least the halfway point of an officeholder's term;
- required public disclosure of all PAC fund-raising letters;
- mandatory revelation of administrative costs in all PAC solicitation materials;
- universal reporting of candidate selections by each PAC to its membership;
- severe restrictions on honoraria and special-interest-paid travel for congressmen;
- elimination of some congressmen's golden parachute retirement funds.

This comprehensive agenda will accomplish the six essential objectives outlined as goals for this program in the introduction. Free media time clearly reduces fund-raising pressure on candidates by subtracting from campaign costs without the damaging side effects of artificially restricting actual campaign communications. Challengers benefit as much or more than incumbents from many of these changes (including free media time and the tax credit schemes), thus maintaining or even increasing the competitiveness of campaigns. The tax credits also have great potential for broadening the base of small contributors and increasing public participation in campaign financing.

Many of these proposals would build the vital stabilizing institutions of American politics, the parties. Strengthened parties, in turn, would help to check and indirectly limit the influence of special interest groups. Increasing the base of individual donors also works toward the same goal. Finally, the major elements of real and quasi corruption (deceit by some PACs, honoraria, and so on) can be exposed, in part by mandating fuller disclosure and in part by eliminating them.

All of these proposals are designed to produce a better political system and a more informative campaign process. But no goal is more vital than the restoration of public confidence in that system and that process. The many charges of corruption that have been raised in the past two decades—some accurate and some not—have almost certainly increased the level of public cynicism about politics and battered the voters' trust in the fairness of American government. That is why it is of critical importance for the *next* set of campaign finance reforms to solve real problems instead of imagined ones. While the perception of corruption is often as detrimental as the real thing, reforms must address the actual wrong-doings first.

A clear-eyed understanding of the limits of reform and a deep appreciation for constitutional freedoms that cannot be abridged will be required to create a *workable,* as well as an ethical, system of campaign finance. By contrast, if we focus on the wrong targets or insist on unrealistic perfection and purity, then we will treat symptoms and not causes and will merely create another jerry-built rig of good intentions and unintended consequences. The rig's eventual, inevitable collapse will increase public cynicism still further, making responsible, effective reform even more difficult to achieve.

Notes

Introduction

1. See Michael Johnston, *Political Corruption and Public Policy in America* (Monterey, Calif.: Brooks/Cole, 1982); and John Thomas Noohan, *Bribes* (New York: Macmillan, 1984).

2. Jay M. Shafritz, *The Dictionary of American Government and Politics* (Chicago: Dorsey, 1988), pp. 141-42.

3. William Riordan, ed., *Plunkitt of Tammany Hall* (New York: Dutton, 1963).

4. 96 S.Ct. 612 (1976).

Chapter 1

1. Quotations from Common Cause direct-mail package to members, January 1987.

2. *The Political Report*, August 24, 1984, p. 2.

3. See *Campaign Practices Reports* (Washington, D. C.: Congressional Quarterly, Inc., July 30, 1984), pp. 1-3.

4. *The New Republic*, May 28, 1984, p. 9.

5. For a much more extended discussion of these subjects, see Larry Sabato, *PAC POWER: Inside the World of Political Action Committees*, rev. ed. (New York: W. W. Norton, 1985); and *What Price PACS?* (New York: Report of the Twentieth Century Fund Task Force on Political Action Committees, 1984).

6. Michael J. Malbin, "The Problem of PAC-Journalism," *Public Opinion*, December/January 1983, pp. 15-16, 59.

7. See Larry Sabato, *The Rise of Political Consultants* (New York: Basic Books, 1981); see also *National Journal*, April 16, 1983, pp. 780-81.

8. David Adamany, "The New Faces of American Politics," *The Annals*, July 1986, pp. 31-32.

9. See Frank J. Sorauf, "Accountability in Political Action Committees: Who's in Charge?" (Paper prepared for the annual meeting of the American Political Science Association, Denver, Colo., September 2-5, 1982), pp. 21-22.

10. The random-sample telephone poll of 1,587 adults was taken in September 1983 at about the time of the AFL-CIO endorsement.

11. See Sabato, *PAC POWER,* pp. 122-59, 222-28.

12. See, for example, Edwin M. Epstein, "An Irony of Electoral Reform," *Regulation,* May/June 1979, pp. 35-44; and Christopher Madison, "Federal Subsidy Programs under Attack by Unlikely Marriage of Labor and Right," *National Journal,* December 31, 1983, pp. 2682-84.

13. Elizabeth Drew, "Politics and Money, Part I," *The New Yorker,* December 6, 1982, pp. 38-45.

14. Herbert E. Alexander, *Financing the 1980 Election* (Lexington, Mass.: D.C. Heath, 1983), p. 379.

15. Robert J. Samuelson, "The Campaign Reform Failure," *The New Republic,* September 5, 1983, pp. 32-33.

16. From the NRCC publication "Working with PACs" (1982).

17. See *The Federalist, No. 10,* for a much fuller discussion of the role of factions in a democratic society.

18. Alexis de Tocqueville, *Democracy in America,* vol. 1 (New York: Vintage Books, 1954), p. 224.

19. As quoted in Drew, "Politics and Money," p. 147.

20. Common Cause "If At First You Don't Succeed, Give, Give Again" (Press release, Washington, D.C., March 20, 1987).

21. "Cleaning Up Reform," *Wall Street Journal,* November 10, 1983, p. 26.

22. Finley Peter Dunne, *The World of Mr. Dooley,* edited with an introduction by Louis Filler (New York: Collier Books, 1962), pp. 155-56.

Chapter 2

1. See *PACs and Lobbies,* April 6, 1983, pp. 1-3.

2. The limit applied to House candidates only. For Senate candidates, between $175,000 and $750,000 would have been allowed, depending on the size of the state. Limits for both House and Senate candidates were to be adjusted upward in cases of runoffs and contested primaries. Senator Boren's more extensive 1987 bill

(S.2), introduced with Senator Robert Byrd (D–W. Va.), dealt only with Senate elections and proposed public financing. PACs were to have no role in the general elections of candidates receiving public funds. In the primaries (or primaries *and* general elections of candidates *not* receiving public funding) total PAC gifts could not exceed $175,000 for a Senate candidate from a small state, up to $750,000 for a Senate candidate in the most heavily populated states.

3. Personal interview with the author, Washington, D.C., August 25, 1983.

4. *Campaign Practices Reports,* May 5, 1986, pp. 1-5.

5. Charles R. Babcock and Richard Morin, "Greek Americans, Home State Are Dukakis' Rich Quarry," *Washington Post,* May 29, 1988, p. A1.

6. Quoted in Herbert E. Alexander and Brian A. Haggerty, *The Federal Election Campaign Act: After a Decade of Political Reform* (Washington, D.C.: Citizens' Research Foundation, 1981), p. 74.

7. For example, the Boren bill (S.2 discussed in note 2) also included overall spending ceilings for Senate candidates, geared to each state's voting-age population.

8. A 1978 *National Journal* analysis estimated that the average House member that year received benefits of at least $350,000, compared with about half that amount in 1970; by 1988, the average figure was at least $700,000 after members' mail costs were included. Figures for the Senate have gone from a minimum of $350,000 in 1970 to at least $700,000 in 1978 and $1.4 million in 1988; those totals are nearly twice as high for senators from the most populous states. From Richard E. Cohen, "PACs and Perks," *National Journal,* June 11, 1988, p. 1582.

9. The least-respected and least-obeyed aspect of federal election law may be the state-by-state spending ceilings in the presidential nominating process. For instance, most candidates allocate many expenses for the crucial New Hampshire primary to neighboring Massachusetts using accounting subterfuge, while other candidates simply exceed the limits outright, assuming (correctly) that the Federal Election Commission will not ascertain the violation until much later and will not punish them severely when it does.

10. Philip M. Stern, "No Vote, No Contribution," *Washington Post,* June 12, 1988, p. C5.

Chapter 3

1. Calculated from total 1985–86 congressional financial activity data provided by the Federal Election Commission.

2. Larry Sabato, *PAC POWER: Inside the World of Political Action Committees,* rev. ed. (New York: W. W. Norton, 1985), p. 166.

3. U.S. Congress, House, Subcommittee on Elections, Committee on House Administration, "Hearings on Campaign Finance," 100th Congress, 1st sess. (Washington, D.C.: U.S. Government Printing Office, 1987), pp. 671-75.

4. Based on total expenditures of about $400 million counted by the NAB. Since actual total congressional campaign expenditures in 1985–86 were almost $451 million, one can assume that the NAB estimate of airtime costs should really be closer to $110 million.

5. See Subcommittee on Elections, "Hearings on Campaign Finance," pp. 701-16.

6. Based again on total congressional campaign expenditures in 1985–86 of $451 million. Not included in the estimates cited, of course, are the substantial charges levied for media consulting and the actual production of media advertisements, since these monies are not given to broadcasters.

7. Herbert E. Alexander, *Financing the 1984 Election* (Lexington, Mass.: D.C. Heath, 1986), pp. 304-8, 329-31.

8. Herbert E. Alexander and Brian A. Haggerty, "Misinformation on Media Money," *Public Opinion,* May/June 1988, pp. 6-7.

9. See Center for Responsive Politics, "Improving Media Access for Congressional Candidates" (Draft, Washington, D.C., April 22, 1988), pp. 1, 10.

10. Twentieth Century Fund Commission on Campaign Costs in the Electronic Era, *Voters' Time* (New York: Twentieth Century Fund, 1969).

11. Ibid., p. 4.

12. Ibid., p. 5.

13. Ibid., p. 6.

14. Campaign Study Group, "Increasing Access to Television for Political Candidates" (Cambridge, Mass.: Institute of Politics, Har-

vard University, July 20, 1978). See also George H. White, *A Study of Access to Television for Political Candidates* (Cambridge, Mass.: Institute of Politics, Harvard University, May 1978).

15. Center for Responsive Politics, "Improving Media Access," pp. 62-63.

16. Larry Sabato, *The Rise of Political Consultants* (New York: Basic Books, 1981), pp. 179-82, 321-28.

17. Fred Flaxman, a vice president of public station WTTW-TV, Chicago, writing in the *Washington Post,* January 4, 1987, p. C5.

18. Estimates were sought from local broadcasters, and are based on a seventeen-hour average broadcasting day, with about three hours of each day's load comprised of paid commercials.

19. The Center for Responsive Politics disputes the broadcasters' claims, however. See CRP, "Improving Media Access," pp. 48-49.

20. See Larry Sabato, "Parties, PACs, and Independent Groups," in Thomas E. Mann and Norman J. Ornstein, eds., *The American Elections of 1982* (Washington, D.C.: American Enterprise Institute, 1983), pp. 78-79.

21. Ibid., pp. 84-86.

22. Some Republican candidates were reluctant to be tied to a then-unpopular President Reagan in 1982, when the GOP aired its "Stay the Course with Reagan" and "Give the Guy a Chance" ads in the midst of a severe recession.

23. Sabato, *The Rise of Political Consultants,* pp. 293, 300-301, n. 73.

24. See ibid., pp. 157-58, for a Michigan State Republican party example.

25. See, for example, Gary C. Jacobson, *The Politics of Congressional Elections* (Boston: Little, Brown, 1983).

26. Sabato, *The Rise of Political Consultants,* p. 123.

27. "Party political" broadcasts in Great Britain are simulcast, but there are only a handful of national networks.

28. Sabato, *The Rise of Political Consultants,* p. 123.

29. Ibid., pp. 123-43.

30. Commission on Campaign Costs, *Voters' Time,* pp. 51-52.

31. See the legislation cited in Center for Responsive Politics, "Improving Media Access," pp. 55-57.

32. See Sabato, *The Rise of Political Consultants,* chap. 2.

33. Center for Responsive Politics, "Improving Media Access," pp. 69-70.

34. Ibid., pp. 70-73. The Federal Communications Commission (FCC) has recently tried to pump some life back into l.u.r. by requiring (as of August 1987) that preempted political spots *must* be run before the election and in a similar time slot to the one originally scheduled, *if* the broadcasters do similar rescheduling for their most favored commercial customers. Some political media consultants were encouraged by the FCC action, but others doubt the practical effect of the ruling, and some television station managers indicated it would have little impact on their practices. See Lloyd Grove, "TV Epic: Nominees vs. Stations on Ad Rates," *Washington Post,* September 8, 1988, p. A15.

35. Center for Responsive Politics, "Improving Media Access," pp. 84-86.

36. Advisory Commission on Intergovernmental Relations, *The Transformation in American Politics* (Washington, D.C., 1986), pp. 377-79, and Sabato, *The Rise of Political Consultants,* pp. 186-92, 326-28.

37. For example, many candidates are airing spots six months or even a year ahead of the election to shore up support or to "inoculate" themselves against charges likely to be made by their opponents in the general election. We may regret year-round campaigning, but restricting discounted rates to a brief period before the election will not halt the sometimes effective practice of early advertising. However, a lack of discounts will make it more difficult for poorly funded challengers to air any early spots, building in yet another advantage for incumbents. It is surely undesirable to give incumbents any greater edge than they already enjoy—a contention that was more fully discussed earlier in this paper.

38. Advisory Commission on Intergovernmental Relations, *The Transformation in American Politics,* pp. 380-81.

Chapter 4

1. See Larry Sabato, *The Party's Just Begun: Shaping Political Parties for America's Future* (Boston: Little, Brown/Scott Foresman, 1988).

2. See, for example, Doris A. Graber, *Mass Media and American Politics,* 2d ed. (Washington, D.C.: Congressional Quarterly Press, 1984), pp. 135-76.

3. See Larry Sabato, *The Rise of Political Consultants* (New York: Basic Books, 1981), esp. chaps. 1, 3.

4. Supporting data for these conclusions are contained in Sabato, *The Party's Just Begun,* pp. 110-50.

5. 86 Stat. 3 (1971).

6. 93 Stat. 1339 (1979).

7. For more detailed treatment, see Larry Sabato, *PAC Power: Inside the World of Political Action Committees,* rev. ed. (New York: W. W. Norton, 1985), pp. 7-10. See also Joseph E. Cantor, *Campaign Financing in Federal Elections: A Guide to the Law and Its Operation* (Washington, D.C.: Library of Congress Congressional Research Service Report no. 86-143 GOV, August 8, 1986); Michael J. Malbin, ed., *Money and Politics in the United States: Financing Elections in the 1980s* (Washington, D.C.: American Enterprise Institute/Chatham House, 1984).

8. This assumes that the party committee or PAC is a multicandidate committee. See Sabato, *PAC Power,* pp. 7-8. If the committee or PAC has not qualified as a multicandidate committee, then a gift of only $1,000 maximum is permitted.

9. Under 2 U.S.C. 441a(d).

10. A 100 percent tax credit would almost certainly increase party giving. The California Commission on Campaign Financing found that 35 percent of state residents would either increase their political gifts or give for the first time if there were a 100 percent credit. See California Commission on Campaign Financing, "The New Gold Rush: Financing California's Legislative Campaigns" (Sacramento: State of California, 1985), p. 15.

11. Only the states of Alaska, Florida, Nevada, South Dakota, Texas, Washington, and Wyoming have no income tax. Minnesota and the District of Columbia already provide a 50 percent tax credit for political contributions.

12. See the polls cited in Sabato, *PAC Power,* pp. 160-63.

13. Cited in Sabato, *The Party's Just Begun,* pp. 213-14.

14. Ibid.

15. See Holly Wagner, "Costly Campaigns Attract Special Interest Dollars," *State Government News,* October 1986, p. 20.

16. Cited in Sabato, *The Party's Just Begun,* p. 215.

17. See David Adamany, "The New Faces of American Politics," *The Annals,* July 1986, pp. 23-24; Herbert E. Alexander, *Financing the 1980 Election* (Lexington, Mass.: D.C. Heath, 1983), p. 422;

John C. Green and James L. Guth, "Partisans and Ideologues: A Profile of Contributors to Party and Ideological PACs" (Paper prepared for the annual meeting of the Southern Political Science Association, Birmingham, Ala., November 3-6, 1983), pp. 11-15; and Ruth S. Jones and Warren E. Miller, "Financing Campaigns: Macro Level Innovation and Micro Level Response," *Western Political Quarterly* (June 1985), pp. 187-210.

It is also worth noting that between 23 and 29 percent of the eligible taxpayers have regularly checked the $1 federal Presidential Election Campaign Fund box. Similar check-offs in the thirteen states that have them have garnered an average 22 percent participation rate (Wagner, "Costly Campaigns Attract Special Interest Dollars," p. 20). Finally, about 7 percent of the federal taxpayers annually took advantage of the 50 percent tax credit when it was available (California Commission on Campaign Financing, "The New Gold Rush," pp. 15-16).

18. See *Congressional Quarterly Almanac 1977* (Washington, D.C.: Congressional Quarterly, Inc. 1978), p. 798; *Congressional Quarterly Almanac 1978* (Washington, D.C.: Congressional Quarterly, Inc., 1979), p. 769; *Congressional Quarterly Almanac 1979* (Washington, D.C.: Congressional Quarterly, Inc., 1980), p. 551.

19. This proposal has also been made by, among others, David E. Price, *Bringing Back the Parties* (Washington, D.C.: Congressional Quarterly Press, 1984), p. 255, and Herbert E. Alexander, "Public Funding of Congressional Campaigns," *Regulation* (January/February 1980), pp. 31-32.

20. See political scientist John Bibby's comments quoted in Advisory Commission on Intergovernmental Relations, *The Transformation in American Politics* (Washington, D.C., 1986), pp. 306-307.

21. Ibid., pp. 298-326. See also Herbert E. Alexander and Mike Eberts, *Public Financing of State Elections: A Data Book and Election Guide to Public Funding of Political Parties and Candidates in Twenty States* (Los Angeles: Citizen's Research Foundation, 1987).

22. States with public funding provisions that channel money through the parties are: California, Idaho, Indiana, Iowa, Kentucky, Maine, North Carolina, Oklahoma, Oregon, Rhode Island, Utah, and Virginia. States that allocate funds directly to candi-

dates are: Alaska, Hawaii, Maryland, Massachusetts, Michigan, Minnesota, Montana, New Jersey, Oklahoma (included in both lists because its statute provides for both disbursements), and Wisconsin. Maryland and Oklahoma's public funding schemes are now defunct. See Advisory Commission on Intergovernmental Relations, *The Transformation in American Politics,* pp. 300-301.

23. Leon Epstein, *Political Parties in the American Mold* (Madison: University of Wisconsin Press, 1986), pp. 328-29.

24. Figures provided by the Federal Election Commission. The percentage of taxpayers using the check-off varies annually, and thus the amount of money deposited in the fund also varies.

25. Ibid. The surplus declined from $177 million in December 1983 to $93 million the next year.

26. Ibid.

27. As quoted in *First Monday* (November/December 1983), p. 9.

Chapter 5

1. As quoted in *Newsweek,* July 18, 1983, p. 11.

2. See Richard P. Conlon, "A New Problem in Campaign Financing . . . and a *Simple* Legislative Solution" (Paper prepared for the annual meeting of the American Political Science Association, Washington, D.C., August 30–September 2, 1984). Conlon also provided the 1984 figure to the author. Individual contributions of all sizes have also declined as a proportion of money raised. Whereas House and Senate candidates secured 61 percent of their funds from individuals in 1978 and 57 percent in 1980, individuals provided only 53 percent in 1982 and 49 percent in 1984.

3. See Edward Roeder, "House Campaign Borrowing Is Corrupting Elections," *Washington Post,* April 14, 1985, p. B1; and "Banks and Political Lending," *Washington Post* editorial, April 16, 1985, p. A18.

4. David Adamany, "PACs and the Democratic Financing of Politics," *Arizona Law Review* 22, no. 2 (1980): 597-98.

5. See Thomas B. Edsall, "Breakfast with the Senate Finance Chairman—for $10,000," *Washington Post,* February 3, 1987, p. A4; and Edsall, "Bentsen Decides to Disband His $10,000 Breakfast Club," *Washington Post,* February 7, 1987, p. A1. As it happened, Bentsen's benefactors eventually recontributed almost all the money to the senator. But Bentsen paid a political price for

these redonations, too, when their disclosure embarrassed him anew after his selection as the 1988 Democratic vice presidential nominee.

6. See the *Washington Post,* February 6, 1987, p. A1, 6; February 27, 1987, p. A25; March 4, 1987, p. A18.

7. See Sabato, *The Rise of Political Consultants,* pp. 220-67. See also Gregg Easterbrook, "Junk Mail Politics," *The New Republic,* April 25, 1988, pp. 17-21.

8. Robert Timberg, "The PAC Business," *Baltimore Sun,* a series of articles that ran during July 11-19, 1982.

9. See Steven Waldman, "The Hiroshima Hustle," *The Washington Monthly* 18 (October 1986): 35-40; and John Robinson, "Problem PACs: Groups Take in More than They Contribute," *The Boston Globe,* October 2, 1986, pp. 1, 6.

10. See Thomas B. Edsall, "Firms, Lobbies Provide Much of Democrats' Funds," *Washington Post,* August 12, 1986; and Edsall, "Corporate Chiefs Put Heart into Contributions to GOP," *Washington Post,* August 29, 1986.

11. Steve Goldberg, "Big Donations Have a Return: Many Perks at Conventions," *Richmond Times-Dispatch,* June 16, 1988, p. A10.

12. Ibid. The GOP's "Eagles" (contributors of $10,000 or more annually) are chosen for that party's access honors.

13. Democratic presidential candidates Gary Hart and Bruce Babbitt and Republican candidates Jack Kemp and Pat Robertson have all maintained tax-exempt foundations in recent years. Robertson's Freedom Council, which was dissolved in October 1986, has perhaps been the most controversial. See *Washington Post,* June 7, 1986, p. A4, and June 9, 1986, p. A20; and *The New York Times,* December 10, 1986, p. 1.

14. The FEC—intentionally starved and hamstrung by Congress to keep it relatively toothless—needs an infusion of funds even if no new responsibilities are added. Among other things, disclosure (particularly as election day approaches) needs to be more prompt and accessible, but the FEC currently lacks the resources to accomplish this.

15. See Herbert E. Alexander, *"Soft Money" and Campaign Financing* (Washington, D.C.: Public Affairs Council, 1986).

16. See Thomas B. Edsall, "Firms, Lobbies Provide Much of Democrats' Funds," *Washington Post,* August 12, 1986, pp. A1, 8;

and Edsall, "Corporate Chiefs Put Heart into Contributions to GOP," *Washington Post,* August 29, 1986, pp. A1, 10. See also Ronald Brownstein and Maxwell Glen, "Money in the Shadows," *The National Journal,* March 15, 1986, pp. 632-37; *Campaign Practices Reports,* July 14, 1986, p. 3; and Steven Emerson, "Soft Money Hits Hard in '86 Races," *U.S. News and World Report,* July 21, 1986, p. 18.

17. See Steve Goldberg, "Loophole Begets Infusion of 'Soft Money'" *Richmond Times-Dispatch,* June 7, 1988, p. C5; "Soft Money: Report It," *Washington Post* editorial, May 30, 1988, p. A26; Charles R. Babcock, "Fall Race May Cost Twice Amount of Public Funds," *Washington Post,* June 27, 1988, p. A1.

18. *Campaign Practices Reports,* June 13, 1988, p. 7; Charles R. Babcock, "For '86 Races in 5 States, $3.3 million 'Soft Money,'" *Washington Post,* June 14, 1988, p. A4; "Mr. Keating's Soft Money," *Washington Post* editorial, June 15, 1988, p. A22.

19. See Burt Solomon, "Bite-Sized Favors," *The National Journal,* October 11, 1986, pp. 2418-22; Common Cause, "Fee Speech," (Press release, Washington, D.C., August 3, 1988); and Charles R. Babcock, "Hill Lawmakers Find Tax Haven in Honoraria," *Washington Post,* August 7, 1988, pp. A1, 20.

20. Jerald V. Halvorsen, vice president for government affairs at the American Trucking Association, as quoted in Solomon, "Bite-Sized Favors."

21. *Campaign Practices Reports,* June 13, 1988, p. 4; Eric Pianin and Don Phillips, "Lawmakers Disclose Fees for Speeches," *Washington Post,* May 26, 1988, p. A9.

22. David S. Cloud, "Leaders, Tax Experts Top Hill Honoraria Rolls," *Congressional Quarterly Weekly,* June 11, 1988, pp. 1572-74. See also "The 1985 Honoraria Scorecard," *Common Cause Magazine,* July/August 1986, p. 42.

23. Associated Press dispatch, June 11, 1988.

24. Ibid.

25. See Sheila Kaplan, "Join Congress—See the World," *Common Cause Magazine,* September/October 1986, pp. 17-23; and Eric Pianin and Charles R. Babcock, "Congress' Business Vacations," *Washington Post,* June 20, 1988, p. A1.

26. Ibid.

27. Members of Congress can accept travel reimbursements for

speaking, visiting a company plant, participating in a legislative-oriented conference, or even taking part in a celebrity sports tournament. The sponsoring group can be charged expenses for a spouse or an aide as well. While congressmen can accept only a $2,000 honorarium for an appearance, charges for expenses (e.g., travel, lodging, food) are essentially unlimited.

28. Jean Cobb, "The Power of the Purse," *Common Cause Magazine,* May/June 1988, pp. 12-18.

29. See Kevin Chaffee, "Money under the Mattress: What Congressmen Don't Spend," *Washington Monthly,* September 1984, pp. 32-38.

30. Congressmen must pay tax on any campaign money converted to personal use—but not on loans.

31. Chaffee, "Money under the Mattress," pp. 36-37.

32. As quoted in ibid., p. 37.

33. To reduce administrative costs, pro rata refunds of contributions could be limited to those who gave more than a nominal amount (perhaps $100).

34. Cobb, "The Power of the Purse," pp. 14, 18.

35. Testimony of Senator Paul S. Sarbanes (R–Md.), in U.S. Congress, Senate, Committee on Rules and Administration, *Hearing on the Federal Election Campaign Act of 1971,* 98th Congress, 1st sess., p. 157.

36. As quoted in Herbert E. Alexander and Brian A. Haggerty, *The Federal Election Campaign Act: After a Decade of Political Reform* (Washington, D.C.: Citizens' Research Foundation), p. 86.

37. For a background discussion of independent expenditures, see Rodney Smith, "Federal Election Law, Part II: What You Can Get Away With," *Campaigns and Elections,* Fall 1982, p. 22. See also Herbert E. Alexander, *Financing the 1980 Election* (Lexington, Mass.: D.C. Heath, 1983), pp. 129, 168, 370, 378, 387-90.

38. See Alexander, *Financing the 1980 Election,* p. 388; and *The National Journal,* December 17, 1983, p. 2631. In March 1985 the Supreme Court upheld a lower court ruling that declared unconstitutional the $1,000 limitation on independent spending by a PAC in a presidential election. (*FEC v. NCPAC,* 105 Sup. Ct. 1459 [1985]).

39. 96 S. Ct. 612 (1976) or 424 U.S. 1 (1976).

40. This was one provision of the "Clean Campaign Act of 1983,"

H.R. 2490. Senator David Boren's 1986 reform amendment contained a somewhat similar provision. See *Congressional Quarterly Weekly,* August 16, 1986, pp. 1887-90; and *Campaign Practices Reports,* August 13, 1986, pp. 1-4.

41. Personal interview with the author, Washington, D.C., September 21, 1983.

42. See Frank J. Sorauf, "Caught in a Political Thicket: The Supreme Court and Campaign Finance," *Constitutional Commentary,* Winter 1986, pp. 97-121; Richard E. Cohen, "Spending Independently," *The National Journal,* December 6, 1986, pp. 2932-34; Maxwell Glen, "Spending Independently," *The National Journal,* June 21, 1986, pp. 1533-37; *The Political Report,* July 18, 1986, pp. 13-14.

Index

Accountability, 20-21, 45, 64, 69, 70,
Adamany, David, 12, 61
Administrative costs, 55, 72
AFL-CIO, 12
Anderson, John B., 37

Babbitt, Bruce, 84n13
Baltimore Sun, 63
Bentsen, Lloyd, 62
Boren, David, 19, 20, 21, 77n7, 87n40
Bribery, 2
Broadcasting industry, 30, 39, 40. *See also* Media
Brock, William, 53
Buckley v. Valeo (1976), 4, 70
Building fund, 64
Byrd, Robert, 77n2

California, 52, 66, 81n10
Campaign contributions, 21-22, 23-24, 47, 59-61, 68-69; corruption, 3; limits on, 19-20, 43, 49, 51, 71, 72. *See also* Individual gifts; Small donations; Soft money
Campaign costs, 1, 5, 7, 11, 26, 49. *See also* Congressional elections, costs of; Expenditures; Presidential elections, costs of

Campaign Practices Reports, 21
Candidate selection, 12, 47-48, 70, 72
Carter, Jimmy, 27, 37, 54
Center for Responsive Politics, 28, 41, 66
Challengers, 11-12; advantages for, 60-61, 72; disadvantages for, 19-20, 22, 24, 39, 60, 80n37
Cheney, Richard, 60
"Citizens Against PACs" (organization), 23
Coelho, Tony, 54
Colorado, 66
Commission on Campaign Costs in the Electronic Era. *See* Twentieth Century Fund Commission on Campaign Costs in the Electronic Era
Common Cause (organization), 9, 66, 67, 71
Communication. *See* Political communication
Congressional elections, 28-29; costs of, 11, 26, 33-34; expenditures for, 49, 50; funding of, 49, 59, 60, 61, 77n2
Congress members, 66-69; and PACs, 9, 10, 11, 13-15, 17-18
Conservatives, 24, 52
Constituents. *See* Electorate

Contents of media advertising, 30, 34-36
Corruption, 1, 2-5, 7, 65-66, 67, 71, 73. *See also* Pseudo corruption; Quasi corruption; Real corruption

Debts of candidates, 61
Democratic National Convention, 64
Democratic party, 9, 31-32, 54, 56, 57, 65
Democrats, 9, 11, 20, 52, 55, 63, 66
Direct mail fundraising, 12, 49, 53, 63-64, 70, 72
Disclosure of contributions, 5-6, 61-64, 65, 70, 72, 73
Dolan, John "Terry," 69
Dole, Robert, 16
Donations. *See* Campaign contributions
Drew, Elizabeth, 14
Dukakis, Michael, 21
Dunne, Finley Peter, 18

Education, 48
Eisenhower, Dwight, 4
Elections, 16, 34, 65; competitiveness of, 5-6, 22, 34, 59-60. *See also* Congressional elections; Presidential elections
Electoral security, 55, 62
Electorate, 48; influence on legislative voting, 14-15, 16
Eligibility, for free media advertising, 37-39; for public funding, 50, 59-61
Expenditures, 69-71; ceilings on, 1, 6, 9, 22-23, 49-50, 60, 71, 77n7
Fahrenkopf, Frank, 53, 56

FEC. *See* Federal Election Commission
FECA. *See* Federal Election Campaign Act
Federal Communications Commission, 80n34
Federal Election Campaign Act (FECA), 36-37, 38, 40, 48, 49, 65, 68
Federal Election Campaign Fund, 53, 56, 72
Federal Election Commission (FEC), 26, 61-62, 63, 64, 65, 70, 77n9
Federal government, 45
Federalist No. 10, 15
First Amendment, 4, 70
Florida, 66
Formats of media advertising, 30, 34-36
Foundations, 64
Franks, Martin I., 21
Fundraising, 1, 5, 25, 54, 65, 70; fraud in, 63. *See also* Direct mail fundraising

Glenn, John, 12
Golden parachute (congressional), 1, 68-69, 72
Goldwater, Barry, 9, 70
GOP. *See* Republican party
Grantees, of free media advertising, 29
Grassroots campaign contributions, 5, 53, 55

Hart, Gary, 84n13
Harvard Institute of Politics, 28
Honoraria for members of Congress, 3, 66-68, 69, 72
House of Representatives, 14, 67, 68

Income tax, 51, 52-53, 66-67, 72
Incumbents, 47, 55, 62, 72; advantages for, 5, 11, 19-20, 22, 24, 39, 46, 60, 61, 80n37
Independent expenditures, 69-71
Individual gifts, 5, 7-8, 21, 50, 64-66, 73; limits on, 43, 49, 51, 72
Individual rights, 6, 7, 45, 47
Inflation, 43, 50
Institutional advertising, 31-33, 34, 42
Integrity, impairment of, 3-4. See also Corruption
Interest groups, 1, 5, 10, 46; influence of, 3, 7, 23, 51. See also Political Action Committees
Iowa, 55-56
Issue identification, 44, 46, 47, 48

Jacobs, Andrew, 68-69

Kemp, Jack, 84n13
Kirk, Paul, 54
Knox, Frank, 27

Labor, and elections, 12, 56
Legislation, 10, 18, 48, 50
Legislative voting, influences on, 4, 13-15
Liberals, 24, 52, 63

Madison, James, 15
Maine, 52
Malbin, Michael, 10
Markey, Edward, 63
Massachusetts, 9, 52, 63
McGovern, George, 70
Media, 10; influence of, 46, 47
Media advertising, 70-71, 72; costs of, 11, 26-27, 40-42; segment length, 29, 34-36

Missouri, 66
Mondale, Walter, 12, 27, 37
Montana, 52

Nader, Ralph, 14
Name recognition. See Personality politics
National Association of Broadcasters (NAB), 26
National Committee for Peace in Central America, 63
National Conservative Political Action Committee (NCPAC), 69, 71
National Republican Congressional Committee, 15
NCPAC. See National Conservative Political Action Committee
News media. See Media
New York City, 2
New York State, 38
Nomination of candidates. See Candidate selection
Nonresident contributions, 23-24, 71
North Carolina, 55

Obey, David, 22
Obey-Railsback bill, 19
Objectives, in campaign finance reform, 6-8
O'Neill, Thomas P. "Tip," 31-32
Oversight, 4-5

PACs. See Political Action Committees
Party affiliation, 44-45, 47-48
Party committees, 49, 50, 53, 56-57
Party identification, 44, 45, 46, 47-48

Party leadership, 33, 56
Party loyalty, 14
Party politics, 5, 32-33
Personality politics, 5, 22, 46, 47, 61
Plunkitt, George Washington, 2-3
Pluralistic society, 15-16
Political Action Committees (PACs), 4, 46, 50, 63-64; criticism of, 9, 10, 43, 63; influence of, 1, 13-15, 51; limits on, 49, 57, 71, 72
Political communication, 7, 11, 34, 52-53, 60
Political consultants, 46, 47
Political parties, 7, 10; role of, 43-45, 70. See also Democratic party; Republican party; Third parties; Two-party system
Political power, 44, 45, 47-48, 53-54, 55
Political stability, 44-45, 72-73
Preemptible time (advertising), 41-42
Presidential Campaign Fund Act, 70
Presidential elections, expenditures for, 49-50, 77n9; funding of, 54, 65, 70; and media advertising, 26-28
Pseudo corruption, 2, 3-5, 6, 7
Public Affairs Council, 17
Public Citizen (organization), 14
Public financing of candidates, 54-57, 59-60, 71, 77n2
Public interest groups. See Interest groups
Public opinion polls, 12, 38, 51-52, 53

Quasi corruption, 2, 3, 7

Rates, for media advertising, 40-42
Reagan, Ronald, 27, 32, 37, 79n22
Real corruption, 2-3, 7
Representatives, 10, 66, 67
Republican National Convention, 64
Republican party (GOP), 31-32, 54, 56, 65
Republicans, 11, 52, 55, 66, 79n22
Retirement of members of Congress, 1, 68
Robertson, Pat, 84n13
Rogers, Will, 11
Roosevelt, Theodore, 54

Salaries of members of Congress, 66, 68
Samuelson, Robert, 14
Sarbanes, Paul, 69
Senate, 62, 66, 68
Senators, 46, 66, 67; and PACs, 9, 10, 11, 17-18
Seniority system (in Congress), 24
Single-issue politics, 46, 47, 48
Small donations, 7-8, 49, 60, 61
Soft money, 20-21, 64-66
Sorauf, Frank J., 12
Special interests. See Interest groups; PACs
State parties, 50, 54, 55-56, 65, 66
States, and public funding, 55-56
Stern, Philip M., 23-24
"Stop the Baby Killers" (organization), 63
Subsidies, 28, 40, 48, 50. See also Public financing
Suffrage, 16
Supreme Court, 4, 70

"Talking heads" advertising, 35-36

Tax credits, 40, 51-52, 60-61, 70, 72

Taxation, 14. *See also* Income tax

Third parties, 59; and free media advertising, 27, 30, 31, 36-39

Timberg, Robert, 63

Time allotment, for free media advertising, 28, 29, 31, 35, 37, 38

Tocqueville, Alexis de, 16

Travel, by members of Congress, 3, 67, 72

Turnover in Congress, 11, 17-18

Twentieth Century Fund Commission on Campaign Costs in the Electronic Era, 27, 31, 34, 35, 37, 39-40

Two-party system, 7, 16-17, 43, 44, 46, 47

U. S. Committee Against Nuclear War, 63

Values, 45

Virginia, 52

Voter information, 6, 42, 44, 52-53, 61, 62

Voting, influences on, 34, 35, 44

Wall Street Journal, 18

Washington Post, 21

Washington state, 66

Watchdog groups, 4-5, 16

Wealthy candidates, 20, 46

Wertheimer, Fred, 71